The Complete Guide to
DECKS

Updated 4th Edition • Includes the Newest
Products & Fasteners • Add an Outdoor Kitchen

**Creative Publishing
international**

MINNEAPOLIS, MINNESOTA
www.creativepub.com

Library of Congress Cataloging-in-Publication Data

The complete guide to decks. -- Updated 4th ed.
    p. cm.
  At head of title: Black & Decker.
  "Includes the newest products & fasteners; add an outdoor kitchen."
  Includes bibliographical references and index.
  Summary: "Teaches the process of designing, building and main-
taining a deck. Includes the latest contemporary options, such as
how to work with eco-friendly wood and reclaimed plastic"--Provided
by publisher.
  ISBN-13: 978-1-58923-412-3 (soft cover)
  ISBN-10: 1-58923-412-X (soft cover)
  1. Decks (Architecture, Domestic)--Design and construction--
Amateurs' manuals. I. Black & Decker Corporation (Towson, Md.)
II. Creative Publishing International. III. Title: Black & Decker, the
complete guide to decks.
  TH4970.C645 2009
  690'.893--dc22

                                   2008039012

NOTICE TO READERS

For safety, use caution, care, and good judgment when following the procedures described in this book. The publisher and Black & Decker cannot assume responsibility for any damage to property or injury to persons as a result of misuse of the information provided.

The techniques shown in this book are general techniques for various applications. In some instances, additional techniques not shown in this book may be required. Always follow manufacturers' instructions included with products, since deviating from the directions may void warranties. The projects in this book vary widely as to skill levels required: some may not be appropriate for all do-it-yourselfers, and some may require professional help.

Consult your local building department for information on building permits, codes, and other laws as they apply to your project.

The Complete Guide to Decks
Created by: The Editors of Creative Publishing international, Inc., in cooperation with Black & Decker. Black & Decker® is a trademark of The Black & Decker Corporation and is used under license.

Introduction

A deck is an excellent tool for extending the living space of your home into the outdoors while offering a good return on your investment. But perhaps best of all, you can build a spectacular deck all by yourself, regardless of your do-it-yourself experience, as long as you have the know-how. This fully revised and updated edition of *The Complete Guide to Decks* offers everything you'll need to design and build your dream deck correctly and safely—the first time.

The book begins with a gallery of beautiful decks to help get your creative juices flowing. The next chapter will walk you through each phase of the planning and design process. You'll learn how to evaluate your deck site options, interpret important building codes, draft plans, and get a quick tutorial of deck-building basics.

Next, you'll find an in-depth guide to the entire building process, with each chapter focused on a major deck component: erecting structural support, laying decking, constructing stair systems, and installing railings. To conclude the construction portion of the book, we'll show you how to finish (or refinish) your dream deck as well as how to make repairs as the deck ages.

With very few exceptions, building a deck requires a hard plan and detailed drawings. There are many sources for these plans, including the last section of this book. In it you will find ten complete deck plans, each with measured drawings and step-by-step instructions. You will also see several step-by-step projects for customizing your deck, such as turning an underdeck area into a functional screen patio, installing a hot tub or transforming your deck into an impressive outdoor kitchen or entertaining space.

In the final section of the book, we'll help you ramp up your tool collection for building a deck by discussing both common and specialty tools that can give you a leg up in deck building. This section also provides essential information about building materials, including structural lumber, wood or composite decking options, fasteners, connecting hardware, and concrete.

With the help of this comprehensive book, you will be able to build a beautiful, long-lasting deck just the way you like it—safely, quickly, and economically. We're confident you'll see why *The Complete Guide to Decks* continues to be the premiere deck-building manual for do-it-yourselfers and pros alike.

Gallery of Inspiring Decks

Like any major home improvement project, a deck should be designed to suit your family's lifestyle while it improves the value and beauty of your home. Realistically, you should build your deck with a budget in mind. But, a budget doesn't have to squelch your freedom to dream about that ideal new outdoor space. As you begin to plan your project, let your imagination inspire its design. A deck doesn't have to be boring, even if you are a novice do-it-yourselfer or are working with limited finances. A curved metal railing, some attractive lighting or just decking laid in an eye-catching geometric pattern can transform what might otherwise look like a boat dock on stilts into a compelling feature of your yard and neighborhood.

The following gallery of stunning decks is intended to help you explore the possibilities of what your deck could be. Granted, the bigger the deck the more it will cost, but even a small deck that doesn't suit your needs is an expensive investment in the end if you never use it. So, whatever your budget may be, let these images serve as a way to gather ideas. Who knows…one small aspect of an elegant design could be just the key to unlocking the perfect deck plan for your home. Now is your chance to let any and all ideas be fair game.

Decks aren't limited to flat property lots. A carefully designed multi-level deck can traverse even steep slopes, turning them into useful outdoor living spaces.

When designing your new deck, dare to think outside the usual "box." Here, custom railings, a curved platform and two-tone color scheme dramatically improve what would otherwise be a conventional, single-level deck.

Be creative when designing your new deck. A small water feature like this one, situated in the middle of the deck, will definitely get noticed!

A raised platform, large planters and a unique arbor help to set off a portion of this deck and create an intimate space for conversation or dining.

At its essence, a deck is really just a giant wooden platform. Yours will make a more lasting impression if you choose clear, high-quality decking installed with hidden fasteners.

This deck blends harmoniously with the adjacent pond, thanks in part to the lack of a railing and a curved perimeter. Even the deck chair umbrellas mimic the roof lines beyond—subtle touches that contribute to a more organic and unified space.

The large and dramatic accent lighting installed in this deck platform will surely draw family and friends out onto the deck at night. These light fixtures also highlight the planting bed in a way that's different from daytime viewing.

Decking doesn't have to run in parallel rows from one end of a deck to the other. Here, a herringbone pattern of contrasting woods is an engaging way to break the monotony with a dash of geometry.

Low, subtle accent lighting and candles are better ways to illuminate a deck than bright, spotlight-style yard lights. They create a relaxed ambiance with just the right amount of light.

Custom railings give your deck a distinctive look and set it apart from the rest of the neighborhood. Contoured metal balusters and faux stone posts are combined to good effect on this deck to create a sturdy, elegant railing system.

Mixing colorful flowers and brightly painted patio furniture is a low-cost way to make even a small deck more appealing.

Traditional wooden railings are easy to build and accommodate all rectilinear deck styles. You can buy prefabricated, pressure-treated posts and balusters from any home center, or make them from the same lumber you're using for the rest of the deck.

A simple addition to your deck, such as a set of swinging gates, might be all it takes to add a custom flair to your design and add a measure of safety, too.

If you build a second-story deck, keep in mind that the space underneath need not go to waste. By adding a few screened walls and a door, you'll create a bug-free porch with shade to spare. Or add sheathing and siding for a garden shed.

If you have room for it, an expansive deck could become the multipurpose room you've always wanted — for sunning, dining, a hot tub or entertaining larger groups. You are only limited by your imagination and budget.

Composite decking materials can help you create new and exciting shapes for your deck. This leaf-shaped deck proves that "straight and square" is no longer a design limitation.

If your new deck will be exposed to full sun most of the time, consider adding a gazebo, sunshade, or other sheltered feature to it. You'll improve your deck's livability when summer's heat is at its worst.

Do-it-yourself underdeck drain systems can route water away from this area and turn it into dry, usable space. In this example, a finished ceiling, concealed drainage system, and fans help convert the under-deck area into a sheltered patio.

Deck-building materials continue to improve every year. Here, composite decking with faux wood grain is a convincing alternative to real wood, and it will last much longer. Hidden decking fasteners keep deck boards free of nail or screwheads.

FREESTANDING DECKS

Decks which are freestanding do not utilize the exterior wall of an existing house to support vertical loads. If there is an additional beam with posts provided at or within 1/4 of the joist span from the house, as recommended to minimize required lateral load resistance, DECK POST FOOTINGS SHALL BE PLACED AT

Figure 21: Free-Standing Deck

rim joist

rim joist

beam posts

posts

install diagonals per Figure 22

THE SAME ELEVATION AS THE EXISTING HOUSE FOOTING face figure and isolated house with baseline a cylindrical pier recommended to minimize required lateral basement wall. Beam size is field

DECK STABILITY

Decks greater than 2 feet above grade, shall be with diagonal bracing or be attached to the of the house.

Figure 22: Diagonal Bracing Re

beam

2

2x4, typical

(1) 3/8" diameter thru-bolt with washers, typical

BRACING PERPENDICULAR TO

BRACING PARALLEL TO BEAM

American Wood Council

Deck Planning & Design

One of the benefits of building a deck is that you can create an impressive structure in a relatively short period of time, with even modest tools and skills. It's an exciting project to undertake, but don't let your energy and enthusiasm get the best of you. Without careful planning and design on the front end, your deck project could be frustrating to build, unnecessarily costly, or even dangerous to use when you're through. So, in order to put your best foot forward, plan to spend those first hours of the project at a desk developing a thorough plan.

As you begin the planning process, keep in mind that your deck needs to satisfy four goals: it should meet the functional needs of your household, contribute to your home's curb appeal and property value, fit your project budget, and satisfy local building codes for safety. This chapter will help you familiarize yourself with all four goals so you can build confidently and correctly, the first time. Be sure to spend some time reviewing the deck plans provided on pages 242 to 311 of this book, as well as other published deck plans. You may be able to find the perfect deck for your home without designing it from scratch or by making minor modifications to these plans.

In this chapter:

- Evaluating Your Site
- Deck Construction Codes
- Determining Lumber Size
- Understanding Loads
- Developing Your Deck Plan
- Working with Building Inspectors

Evaluating Your Site

That overused real estate adage about "Location, location, location" definitely applies to decks. Once you build your deck, it'll be there to stay, so choose your site carefully. A deck will be affected by sunlight and shade, prevailing winds and seasonal changes. Those natural factors will influence how and when you use your deck. There are other site-related issues to consider as well. An on-grade deck will reduce the size of your yard, which may or may not be an issue, depending on your needs for gardening, lawn space, or play areas. A raised deck could be perfect for entertaining friends, but it could also bring unwanted shade to a flowerbed underneath or darken a nearby living space.

The size and layout of your property will also impact your choice of deck sites. You may need to build a multi-level deck or a long run of steps to reach the ground of a sloping yard. Will your proposed deck site require you to remove a tree or two to accommodate it, or will you simply build around them? A tall deck could give you new vistas on the neighborhood, but will it encroach on your neighbor's window privacy or put you dangerously close to power lines? These are all factors to keep in mind when settling on the final location of your deck. Make sure the benefits of your deck site outweigh any compromises you may need to make.

Sometimes, the location of your deck already will be dictated by the design of house you live in. This suburban home was built with a patio door intended for deck access. However, you may have more than one site to choose from for your deck, so consider all the options before you commit to a final spot.

Deck Siting Considerations

Natural yard features, such as a steep slope, will impact a deck's layout and access. You may need to build a multi-level deck or a long staircase with a landing to accommodate the changing grade.

If your yard is small, plan the size of your deck carefully. You may have to trade flowerbeds, landscaping, or useable yard space for a deck footprint. How much will you miss the yard you'll lose? Will your deck harmonize with the yard or dominate it?

Large trees will either need to be incorporated into your deck scheme or be removed entirely. Roots could pose challenges for digging footings, and tree canopies will influence how much sunlight reaches the deck.

Keep the sun's path in mind as you consider when you plan to use your deck. East-facing decks will provide a place for warm, sunny breakfasts, but they'll be shaded by mid-day. A west-facing deck offers a great vantage point for watching sunsets, but it could become too warm for afternoon tanning. A south or southwesterly deck usually offers the best compromise for general use.

Before you build a second-floor deck, consider whether your site will compromise your neighbor's privacy, place you too close to power lines, or shade areas of the yard or windows beneath.

Deck Construction Codes

Most decks are relatively simple structures, but even a basic deck project must conform to the requirements of building codes in your area. In fact, virtually every aspect of your new deck—from its location on your property to the design you choose and the materials you buy to build it—all must meet stringent guidelines for safety. Codes vary to some degree from state to state, but they are based on general regulations established by the International Residential Code. Your local building inspector can provide you with a list of the relevant deck codes and help you interpret them so you can create code-compliant plans for your deck project. You may also want to download a free PDF copy of the "Prescriptive Residential Deck Construction Guide" (see Resources, page 315).

The next few pages will provide a survey of some of the more common code requirements for decks, although it is by no means comprehensive. Use this section as a way to familiarize yourself with the code requirements you will probably face as you plan and build your new deck.

Footing diameter and depth is determined by your building official, based on the estimated load of the deck and on the composition of your soil. In regions with cold winters, footings must extend below the frost line. Minimum diameter for concrete footings is 8".

Metal flashings must be used to prevent moisture from penetrating between the ledger and the wall.

Beams may overhang posts by no more than 1 ft. Some local building regulations require that, wherever possible, beams should rest on top of posts, secured with metal post-beam caps.

Engineered beams, such as a laminated wood product or steel girder, should be used on decks with very long joist spans, where standard dimension lumber is not adequate for the load. Engineered beams for decks must be rated for exterior use.

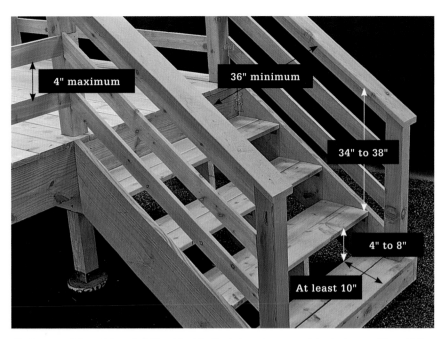

Railings are usually required by local codes for decks more than 30" above the ground and must usually be at least 36" in height. Bottom rails must be positioned with no more than 4" of open space below them. Balusters, whether vertical or horizontal, can be spaced no more than 4" apart.

Stairs must be at least 36" wide. Vertical step risers must be between 4" and 8" and uniform in height within a staircase. Treads must have a horizontal run of at least 10" and be uniform in size within a staircase. Stair railings should be 34" to 38" above the noses of the step treads, and there should be no more than 6" of space between the bottom rail and the steps. The space between the rails or balusters should be no more than 4".

Code violation. The International Building Code no longer allows joists to straddle the sides of a post fastened with through bolts, as shown here. It no longer endorses structural posts made of 4 × 4 lumber: 6 × 6 is the minimum size. Railing posts may be 4 × 4.

Beam assemblies. Deck beams made of 2× lumber must be fastened together with staggered rows of 10d galvanized common nails or #10 wood screws. If the wood components that make up the beam are spliced together, stagger the splices and locate them over beams for added strength.

Post-to-beam attachment. Deck posts, regardless of length or size of deck, should be made of minimum 6 × 6 structural lumber. Notch the posts so that beams can bear fully in the notch, and attach them with pairs of ½-in.-diameter galvanized through bolts and washers. Or, you can mount beams on top of posts with galvanized post cap hardware.

Ledgers and rim joists. When a ledger is fastened to a rim joist, the house siding must be removed prior to installation. Either ½-in.-diameter lag screws or through-bolts with washers can be used to make the connections.

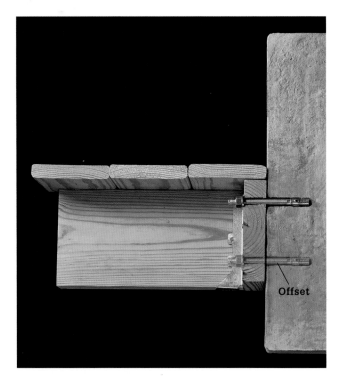

Ledgers and concrete walls. Ledgers fastened to solid concrete must be attached with bolts and washers driven into approved expansion, epoxy or adhesive anchors.

Ledgers and block walls. When fastening ledgers to hollow concrete block walls, the block cells in the ledger attachment areas must be filled with concrete or grout. Secure the attachment bolts to the wall with approved epoxy anchors with washers.

No notched railing posts. Code no longer allows deck railing posts to be notched where they attach to the deck rim joists. Railing posts should be fastened to rim joists with pairs of ½-in.-diameter through bolts and washers. In some cases, hold-down anchor hardware may also be required.

Stair lighting. Deck stairs must be illuminated at night from a light located at the top of the landing. The light can be switch-controlled from inside the house, motion-controlled, or used in conjunction with a timer switch.

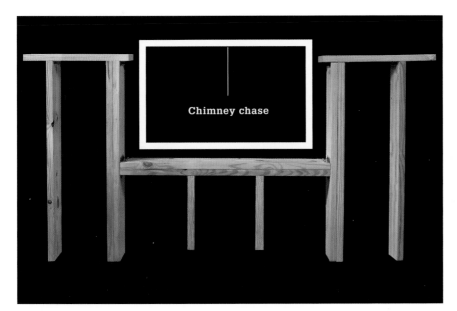

Chimney chases & bays. When framing a deck around a chimney or bay window, a suitable double header must be added where the ledger is spliced to accommodate the obstruction. The header can span a maximum of 6 ft.

Rim joist connections. Attach rim joists to the end of each joist with five #10 × 3-in. minimum wood screws. Secure decking to the top of rim joists with #10 × 3-in. minimum wood screws, spaced every 6 in.

Determining Lumber Size

A deck has seven major structural parts: the ledger, decking, joists, one or more beams, posts, stairway stringers, and stairway treads. To create a working design plan and choose the correct lumber size, you must know the span limits of each part of the deck. The ledger is attached directly to the house and does not have a span limit.

A span limit is the safe distance a board can cross without support from underneath. The maximum safe span depends on the size and wood species of the board. For example, 2 × 6 southern pine joists spaced 16" on-center can safely span 9'9", while 2 × 10 joists can span 16'1".

Begin planning by first choosing the size and pattern for the decking. Use the tables on the opposite page. Then determine the size and layout of the joists and beams, using the information and span tables on page 23. In general, a deck designed with larger-size lumber, like 2 × 12 joists and beams, requires fewer pieces because the boards have a large span limit. Finally, choose the stair and railing lumber that fits your plan, again using the tables on the opposite page.

Use the design plans to make a complete list of the quantities of each lumber size your deck requires. Add 10% to compensate for lumber flaws and construction errors. Full-service lumberyards have a fine lumber selection, but prices may be higher than those at home improvement centers. The quality of lumber at home centers can vary, so inspect the wood and hand-pick the pieces you want or add a larger percentage to compensate for lumber flaws. Both lumberyards and home centers will deliver lumber for a small fee, and you can usually return unused, uncut lumber if you keep your receipts.

Meet or exceed all lumber size codes. For example, use lumber that is at least 6 × 6" for all deck posts, regardless of the size of the deck or the length of the post.

Developing Your Deck Plan

A deck plan is more than just measured drawings. It needs to account for your deck's functional purposes as well as its dimensional form. Before you begin drawing plans, determine everything you want your deck to include. Here's where you'll focus on functional concerns. The size, shape, and location of your deck can be affected by several questions: Will the deck be used for entertaining? Will you do outdoor cooking on it? Do you need privacy? Consider how the features of the house and yard influence the deck design. Weather, time of day, and seasonal changes affect deck usage. For example, if your deck will be used mainly for summertime evening meals, look at the sun, shade, and wind patterns on the planned site during this time of day.

Of course, building plans also help you estimate lumber and hardware needs, and provide the measurements needed to lay out the deck and cut the lumber. You will need two types of drawings for your deck plans and to obtain a building permit. A plan view shows the parts of the deck as they are viewed from directly overhead. An elevation shows the deck parts as viewed from the side or front.

Calculator Conversion Chart ▸

8ths	16ths	Decimal
	1	.0625
1	2	.125
	3	.1875
2	4	.25
	5	.3125
3	6	.375
	7	.4375
4	8	.5
	9	.5625
5	10	.625
	11	.6875
6	12	.75
	13	.8125
7	14	.875
	15	.9375
8	16	1.0

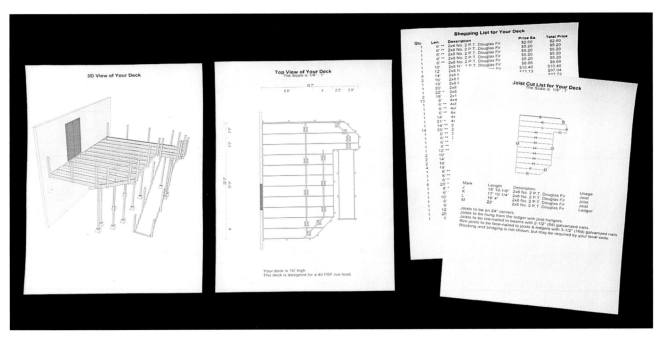

Many building centers will help you design and create deck plan drawings if you purchase your lumber and other deck materials from them. Their design capabilities include determining a detailed lumber and materials list based on the exact deck plan created.

Dimension & Span Limit Tables for Deck Lumber ▸

Nominal vs. Actual Lumber Dimensions: When planning a deck, remember that the actual size of lumber is smaller than the nominal size by which lumber is sold. Use the actual dimensions when drawing a deck design plan.

Nominal	Actual
1 × 4	¾" × 3¾"
1 × 6	¾" × 5¾"
2 × 4	1½" × 3½"
2 × 6	1½" × 5½"
2 × 8	1½" × 7¼"
2 × 10	1½" × 9¼"
2 × 12	1½" × 11¼"
4 × 4	3½" × 3½"
6 × 6	5¼" × 5¼"

Recommended Decking Span Between Joists: Decking boards can be made from a variety of lumber sizes. For a basic deck use 2 × 4 or 2 × 6 lumber with joists spaced 16" apart.

Decking Boards	Recommended Span
1 × 4 or 1 × 6, laid straight	16"
1 × 4 or 1 × 6, laid diagonal	12"
2 × 4 or 2 × 6, laid straight	16"
2 × 4 or 2 × 6, laid diagonal	12"
2 × 4, laid on edge	24"

Minimum Stair Stringer Sizes: Size of stair stringers depends on the span of the stairway. For example, if the bottom of the stairway lies 7 feet from the deck, build the stringers from 2 × 12s. Stringers should be spaced no more than 36" apart. Use of a center stringer is recommended for stairways with more than three steps.

Span of Stairway	Stringer Size
Up to 6 ft.	2 × 10
More than 6 ft.	2 × 12

Recommended Railing Sizes: Sizes of posts, rails, and caps depend on the spacing of the railing posts. For example, if railing posts are spaced 6 feet apart, use 4 × 4 posts and 2 × 6 rails and caps.

Space Between Railing Posts	Post Size	Cap Size	Rail Size
2 ft. to 3 ft.	2 × 4	2 × 4	2 × 4
3 ft. to 4 ft.	4 × 4	2 × 4	2 × 4
4 ft. to 6 ft.	4 × 4	2 × 6	2 × 6

Chart 1: Maximum Spans for Various Joist Sizes ▸

Size	Southern Pine			Ponderosa Pine			Western Cedar		
	12" OC	16" OC	24" OC	12" OC	16" OC	24" OC	12" OC	16" OC	24 OC
2 × 6	10 ft. 9"	9ft. 9"	8 ft. 6	9 ft. 2"	8 ft. 4"	7 ft. 0"	9 ft. 2"	8 ft. 4"	7 ft. 3"
2 × 8	14 ft. 2"	12 ft. 10"	11 ft. 0"	12 ft. 1"	10 ft. 10"	8 ft. 10"	12 ft. 1"	11 ft. 0"	9 ft. 2"
2 × 10	18 ft. 0"	16 ft. 1"	13 ft. 5"	15 ft. 4"	13 ft. 3"	10 ft. 10"	15 ft. 5"	13 ft. 9"	11 ft. 3"
2 × 12	21 ft. 9"	19 ft. 0"	15 ft. 4"	17 ft. 9"	15 ft. 5"	12 ft. 7"	18 ft. 5"	16 ft. 5"	13 ft. 0"

Drawing Deck Plans

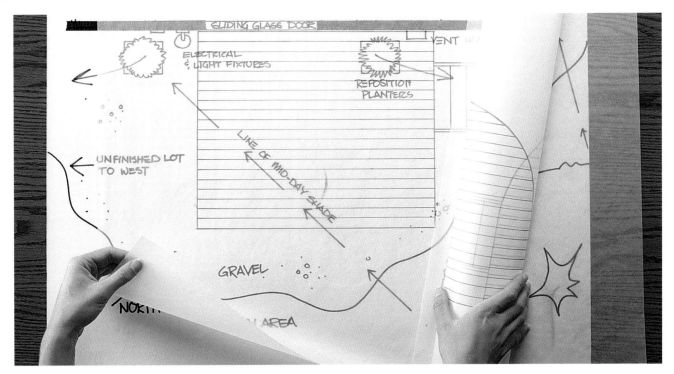

Use tracing paper to sketch different deck layouts. Then, test your ideas by overlaying the deck sketches onto a drawing of your building site. Make sure to consider sun patterns and the locations of existing landscape features when developing a deck plan.

Adapt an existing deck plan, either borrowed from a book or magazine, or purchased in blueprint form. Tracing paper, pens, and measuring tools are all you need to revise an existing deck plan.

Use drafting tools and graph paper if you are creating a deck plan from scratch. Use a generous scale, such as 1" equals 1 ft., that allows you to illustrate the deck in fine detail. Remember to create both overhead plan drawings and side elevation drawings of your project.

How to Create Design Drawings

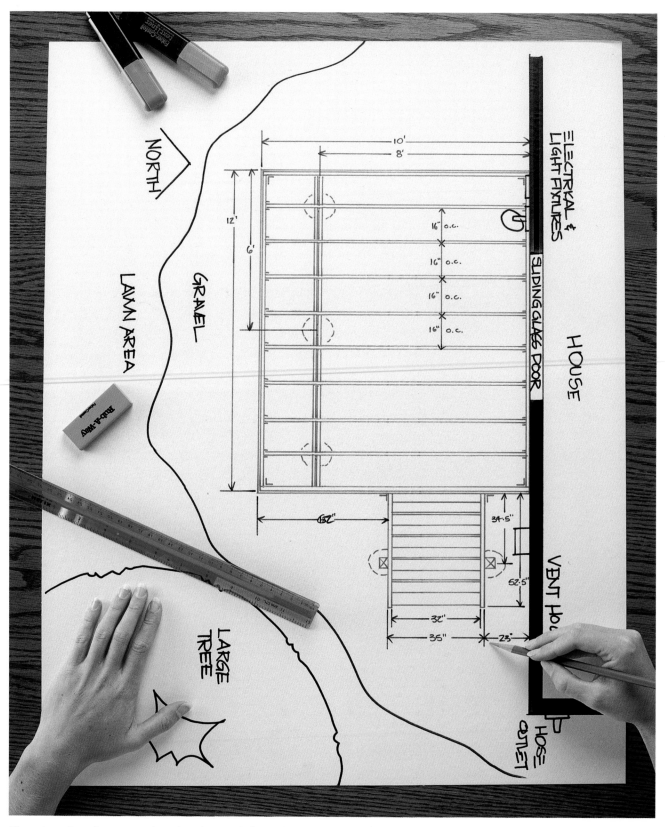

Plan view drawings must show locations and dimensions for ledgers, footings, posts, beams, and joists.

Developing Your Deck Plan

A deck plan is more than just measured drawings. It needs to account for your deck's functional purposes as well as its dimensional form. Before you begin drawing plans, determine everything you want your deck to include. Here's where you'll focus on functional concerns. The size, shape, and location of your deck can be affected by several questions: Will the deck be used for entertaining? Will you do outdoor cooking on it? Do you need privacy? Consider how the features of the house and yard influence the deck design. Weather, time of day, and seasonal changes affect deck usage. For example, if your deck will be used mainly for summertime evening meals, look at the sun, shade, and wind patterns on the planned site during this time of day.

Of course, building plans also help you estimate lumber and hardware needs, and provide the measurements needed to lay out the deck and cut the lumber. You will need two types of drawings for your deck plans and to obtain a building permit. A plan view shows the parts of the deck as they are viewed from directly overhead. An elevation shows the deck parts as viewed from the side or front.

Calculator Conversion Chart ▸

8ths	16ths	Decimal
	1	.0625
1	2	.125
	3	.1875
2	4	.25
	5	.3125
3	6	.375
	7	.4375
4	8	.5
	9	.5625
5	10	.625
	11	.6875
6	12	.75
	13	.8125
7	14	.875
	15	.9375
8	16	1.0

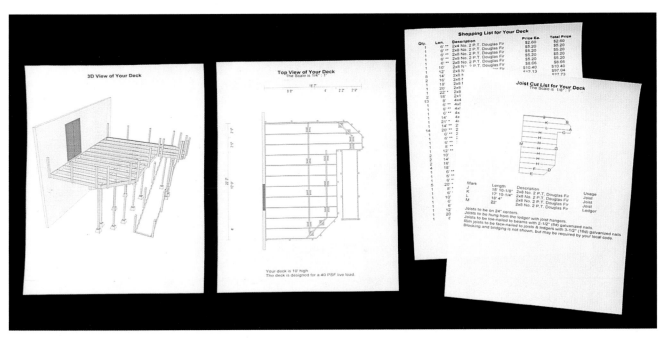

Many building centers will help you design and create deck plan drawings if you purchase your lumber and other deck materials from them. Their design capabilities include determining a detailed lumber and materials list based on the exact deck plan created.

Chart 2: Diameters for Post Footing (inches) ▸

Joist Length		Post Spacing								
		4'	5'	6'	7'	8'	9'	10'	11'	12'
6'	Southern Pine Beam	1–2×6	1–2×6	1–2×6	2–2×6	2–2×6	2–2×6	2–2×8	2–2×8	2–2×10
	Ponderosa Pine Beam	1–2×6	1–2×6	1–2×8	2–2×8	2–2×8	2–2×8	2–2×10	2–2×10	2–2×12
	Corner Footing	6 5 4	7 6 5	7 6 5	8 7 6	9 7 6	9 7 6	10 8 7	10 8 7	10 9 7
	Intermediate Footing	9 8 7	10 8 7	10 9 7	11 9 8	12 10 9	13 10 9	14 11 10	14 12 10	15 12 10
7'	Southern Pine Beam	1–2×6	1–2×6	1–2×6	2–2×6	2–2×6	2–2×8	2–2×8	2–2×10	2–2×10
	Ponderosa Pine Beam	1–2×6	1–2×6	1–2×8	2–2×8	2–2×8	2–2×10	2–2×10	2–2×10	2–2×12
	Corner Footing	7 5 5	7 6 5	8 7 6	9 7 6	9 8 7	10 8 7	10 8 7	11 9 8	11 9 8
	Intermediate Footing	9 8 7	10 8 7	11 9 8	12 10 9	13 11 9	14 11 10	15 12 10	15 13 11	16 13 11
8'	Southern Pine Beam	1–2×6	1–2×6	2–2×6	2–2×6	2–2×8	2–2×8	2–2×8	2–2×10	2–2×10
	Ponderosa Pine Beam	1–2×6	2–2×6	2–2×8	2–2×8	2–2×8	2–2×10	2–2×10	2–2×10	3–2×10
	Corner Footing	7 6 5	8 6 6	9 7 6	9 8 7	10 8 7	10 8 7	11 9 8	11 9 8	12 10 9
	Intermediate Footing	10 8 7	11 9 8	12 10 9	13 11 9	14 11 10	15 12 10	16 13 11	16 13 12	17 14 12
9'	Southern Pine Beam	1–2×6	1–2×6	2–2×6	2–2×6	2–2×8	2–2×8	2–2×8	2–2×10	2–2×12
	Ponderosa Pine Beam	1–2×6	2–2×6	2–2×8	2–2×8	2–2×10	2–2×10	2–2×10	3–2×10	3–2×10
	Corner Footing	7 6 5	8 7 6	9 7 6	10 8 7	10 9 7	11 9 8	12 10 8	12 10 9	13 10 9
	Intermediate Footing	10 9 7	12 10 8	13 10 9	14 11 10	15 12 10	16 13 11	17 14 12	17 14 12	18 15 13
10'	Southern Pine Beam	1–2×6	1–2×6	2–2×6	2–2×6	2–2×8	2–2×8	2–2×10	2–2×12	2–2×12
	Ponderosa Pine Beam	1–2×6	1–2×6	2–2×8	2–2×8	2–2×10	2–2×10	2–2×12	3–2×10	3–2×12
	Corner Footing	8 6 6	9 7 6	10 8 7	10 8 7	11 9 8	12 10 8	12 10 9	13 11 9	14 11 10
	Intermediate Footing	11 9 8	12 10 9	14 11 10	15 12 10	16 13 11	17 14 12	17 14 12	18 15 13	19 16 14
11'	Southern Pine Beam	1–2×6	2–2×6	2–2×6	2–2×8	2–2×8	2–2×10	2–2×10	2–2×12	2–2×12
	Ponderosa Pine Beam	2–2×6	2–2×6	2–2×8	2–2×8	2–2×10	2–2×12	2–2×12	3–2×10	3–2×12
	Corner Footing	8 7 6	9 7 6	10 8 7	11 9 8	12 9 8	12 10 9	13 11 9	14 11 10	14 12 10
	Intermediate Footing	12 9 8	13 11 9	14 12 10	15 12 10	16 13 11	17 14 12	17 14 12	18 15 13	19 16 14
12'	Southern Pine Beam	1–2×6	2–2×6	2–2×6	2–2×8	2–2×8	2–2×10	2–2×10	2–2×12	3–2×10
	Ponderosa Pine Beam	2–2×6	2–2×6	2–2×8	2–2×10	2–2×10	2–2×12	2–2×12	3–2×12	3–2×12
	Corner Footing	9 7 6	10 8 7	10 9 7	11 9 8	12 10 9	13 10 9	14 11 10	14 12 10	15 12 10
	Intermediate Footing	12 10 9	14 11 10	15 12 10	16 13 11	17 14 12	18 15 13	19 16 14	20 16 14	21 17 15
13'	Southern Pine Beam	1–2×6	2–2×6	2–2×6	2–2×8	2–2×8	2–2×10	2–2×10	2–2×12	3–2×10
	Ponderosa Pine Beam	2–2×6	2–2×6	2–2×8	2–2×10	2–2×10	2–2×12	2–2×12	3–2×12	3–2×12
	Corner Footing	9 7 6	10 8 7	11 9 8	12 10 8	13 10 9	13 11 9	14 12 10	15 12 10	15 13 11
	Intermediate Footing	13 10 9	14 12 10	15 13 11	17 14 12	18 15 13	19 15 13	20 16 14	21 17 15	22 18 15
14'	Southern Pine Beam	1–2×6	2–2×6	2–2×6	2–2×8	2–2×10	2–2×10	2–2×12	3–2×10	3–2×12
	Ponderosa Pine Beam	2–2×6	2–2×8	2–2×8	2–2×10	2–2×12	3–2×10	3–2×12	3–2×12	Eng Bm
	Corner Footing	9 8 7	10 8 7	11 9 8	12 10 9	13 11 9	14 11 10	15 12 10	15 13 11	16 13 11
	Intermediate Footing	13 11 9	15 12 10	16 13 11	17 14 12	18 15 13	20 16 14	21 17 15	22 18 15	23 18 16
15'	Southern Pine Beam	2–2×6	2–2×6	2–2×8	2–2×8	2–2×10	2–2×12	2–2×12	3–2×10	3–2×12
	Ponderosa Pine Beam	2–2×6	2–2×8	2–2×8	2–2×10	3–2×10	3–2×10	3–2×12	3–2×12	Eng Bm
	Corner Footing	10 8 7	11 9 8	12 10 8	13 10 9	14 11 10	14 12 10	15 12 11	16 13 11	17 14 12
	Intermediate Footing	14 11 10	15 12 11	17 14 12	18 15 13	19 16 14	20 17 14	21 17 15	22 18 16	23 19 17

Legend:

10	8	7
14	11	10

Soil composition: Clay Sand Gravel

Understanding Loads

The supporting structural members of a deck—the posts, beams, and joists—must be sturdy enough to easily support the heaviest anticipated load on the deck. They must not only carry the substantial weight of the surface decking and railings, but also the weight of people, deck furnishings, and, in some climates, snow.

The charts and diagrams shown here will help you plan a deck so the size and spacing of the structural members are sufficient to support the load, assuming normal use. These recommendations are followed in most regions, but you should still check with your local building official for regulations that are unique to your area. In cases where the deck will support a hot tub or pool, you must consult your local building inspections office for load guidelines.

When choosing lumber for the structural members of your deck, select the diagram below that best matches your deck design, then follow the advice for applying the charts on the opposite page. Since different species of wood have different strengths, make sure to use the entries that match the type of lumber sold by your building center. When selecting the size for concrete footings, make sure to consider the composition of your soil; dense soils require footings with a larger diameter.

Post-and-beam or notched-post deck: Using Chart 1, determine the proper size for your joists, based on the on-center (OC) spacing between joists and the overall length, or span, of the joists (A). For example, if you will be using southern pine joists to span a 12-ft. distance, you can use 2 × 8 lumber spaced no more than 16" apart, or 2 × 10 lumber spaced no more than 24" apart. Once you have determined allowable joist sizes, use Chart 2 to determine an appropriate beam size, post spacing, and footing size for your deck.

Cantilevered deck: Use the distance from the ledger to the beam (A) to determine minimum joist size, and use A + (2 × B) when choosing beam and footing sizes. For example, if your deck measures 9 ft. from ledger to beam, with an additional 3-ft. cantilevered overhang, use 9 ft. to choose a joist size from Chart 1 (2 × 6 southern pine joists spaced 16" apart, or 2 × 8 joists spaced 24" apart). Then, use A + (2 × B), or 15 ft., to find an appropriate beam size, post spacing, and footing size from Chart 2. *Note: If your deck cantilevers more than 18" beyond the support beam, add 1" to the recommended diameter for footings.*

Multiple-beam deck: Use distance A or B, whichever is larger, when determining joist size from Chart 1. For example, if your deck measures 8 ft. to beam #1 and another 4 ft. to beam #2, you can use 2 × 6 southern pine joists. Referring to Chart 2, use the total distance A + B to determine the size of beam #1, the spacing for the posts, and the size of the footings. Use joist length B to determine the size of beam #2, the post spacing, and footing size. For example, with an overall span of 12 ft. (8 ft. to the first beam, 4 ft. to the second), beam #1 could be made from two southern pine 2 × 8s; beam #2, from two 2 × 6s.

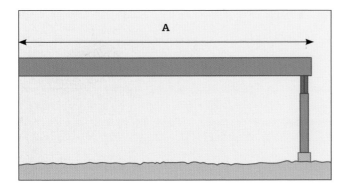

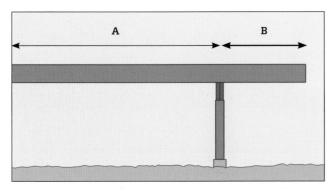

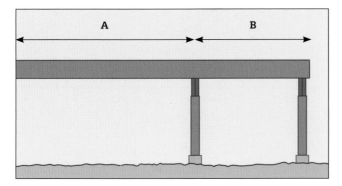

Dimension & Span Limit Tables for Deck Lumber ▸

Nominal vs. Actual Lumber Dimensions: When planning a deck, remember that the actual size of lumber is smaller than the nominal size by which lumber is sold. Use the actual dimensions when drawing a deck design plan.

Nominal	Actual
1 × 4	¾" × 3¾"
1 × 6	¾" × 5¾"
2 × 4	1½" × 3½"
2 × 6	1½" × 5½"
2 × 8	1½" × 7¼"
2 × 10	1½" × 9¼"
2 × 12	1½" × 11¼"
4 × 4	3½" × 3½"
6 × 6	5¼" × 5¼"

Recommended Decking Span Between Joists: Decking boards can be made from a variety of lumber sizes. For a basic deck use 2 × 4 or 2 × 6 lumber with joists spaced 16" apart.

Decking Boards	Recommended Span
1 × 4 or 1 × 6, laid straight	16"
1 × 4 or 1 × 6, laid diagonal	12"
2 × 4 or 2 × 6, laid straight	16"
2 × 4 or 2 × 6, laid diagonal	12"
2 × 4, laid on edge	24"

Minimum Stair Stringer Sizes: Size of stair stringers depends on the span of the stairway. For example, if the bottom of the stairway lies 7 feet from the deck, build the stringers from 2 × 12s. Stringers should be spaced no more than 36" apart. Use of a center stringer is recommended for stairways with more than three steps.

Span of Stairway	Stringer Size
Up to 6 ft.	2 × 10
More than 6 ft.	2 × 12

Recommended Railing Sizes: Sizes of posts, rails, and caps depend on the spacing of the railing posts. For example, if railing posts are spaced 6 feet apart, use 4 × 4 posts and 2 × 6 rails and caps.

Space Between Railing Posts	Post Size	Cap Size	Rail Size
2 ft. to 3 ft.	2 × 4	2 × 4	2 × 4
3 ft. to 4 ft.	4 × 4	2 × 4	2 × 4
4 ft. to 6 ft.	4 × 4	2 × 6	2 × 6

Chart 1: Maximum Spans for Various Joist Sizes ▸

Size	Southern Pine 12" OC	16" OC	24" OC	Ponderosa Pine 12" OC	16" OC	24" OC	Western Cedar 12" OC	16" OC	24 OC
2 × 6	10 ft. 9"	9 ft. 9"	8 ft. 6	9 ft. 2"	8 ft. 4"	7 ft. 0"	9 ft. 2"	8 ft. 4"	7 ft. 3"
2 × 8	14 ft. 2"	12 ft. 10"	11 ft. 0"	12 ft. 1"	10 ft. 10"	8 ft. 10"	12 ft. 1"	11 ft. 0"	9 ft. 2"
2 × 10	18 ft. 0"	16 ft. 1"	13 ft. 5"	15 ft. 4"	13 ft. 3"	10 ft. 10"	15 ft. 5"	13 ft. 9"	11 ft. 3"
2 × 12	21 ft. 9"	19 ft. 0"	15 ft. 4"	17 ft. 9"	15 ft. 5"	12 ft. 7"	18 ft. 5"	16 ft. 5"	13 ft. 0"

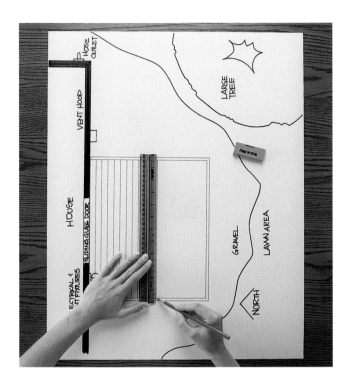
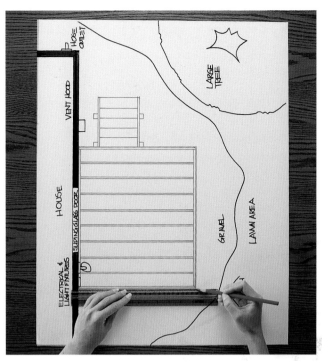

To avoid confusion, do not try to show all parts of the deck in a single plan view, especially for a complicated or multi-level deck. First, draw one plan view that shows the deck outline and the pattern of the decking boards. Then make another plan view (or more) that shows the underlying ledger, joists, beams, and posts.

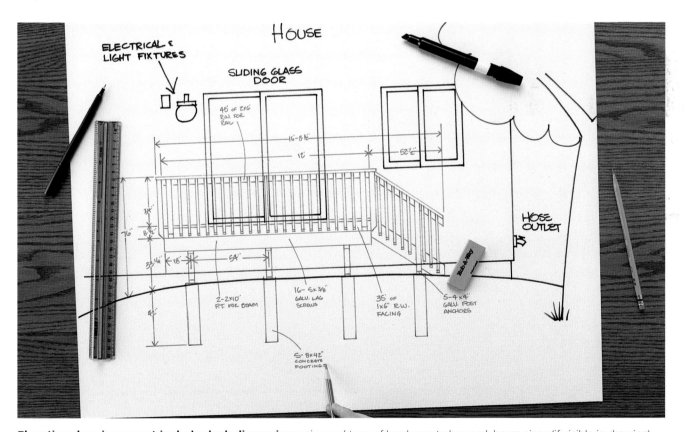

Elevation drawings must include deck dimensions, size and type of hardware to be used, beam sizes (if visible in drawing), and footing locations and their dimensions. Also indicate the grade of the ground in the deck area. Make multiple elevation drawings if necessary for complicated or multi-level decks.

Working with Building Inspectors

In most regions, you must have your plans reviewed and approved by a building official if your deck is attached to a permanent structure or if it is more than 30" high. The building official makes sure that your planned deck meets building code requirements for safe construction.

These pages show some of the most common code requirements for decks. But before you design your project, check with the building inspection division of your city office, since code regulations can vary from area to area. A valuable source of planning information, the building official may provide you with a free information sheet outlining the relevant requirements.

Once you have completed your deck plans, return to the building inspections office and have the official review them. Make certain you know how many copies of the plans they require before you go. If your plans meet code, you will be issued a building permit, usually for a small fee. This process often takes a few days. Regulations may require that a field inspector review the deck at specified stages in the building process. If so, make sure to allow for the review schedule in your project schedule.

While it might be tempting to forge ahead with your deck design and bypass the building inspector entirely, it's a big mistake. Building a deck without the proper permits can lead to fines, and you may even be required to tear the deck down or significantly rebuild it to satisfy local codes. Do the right thing: consider permits and inspections to be a necessary part of the construction process.

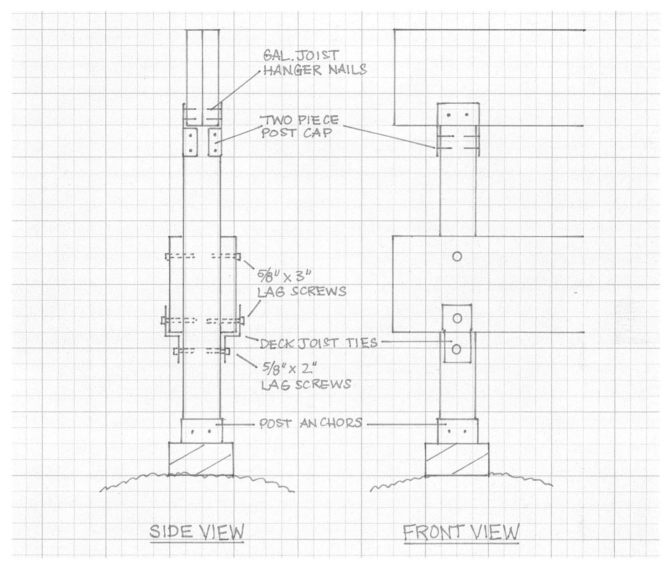

GAL. JOIST
HANGER NAILS

TWO PIECE
POST CAP

5/8" × 3"
LAG SCREWS

DECK JOIST TIES

5/8" × 2"
LAG SCREWS

POST ANCHORS

SIDE VIEW

FRONT VIEW

Draw detailed illustrations of the joinery methods you plan to use on all structural members of your deck. Your building official will want to see details on post-footing connections, post-beam joints, beam-joist joints, and ledger connections. Be prepared to make adjustments. For example, the sandwich method of attaching the lower beams above is no longer endorsed and would likely be flagged.

Plan-approval Checklist ▶

When the building official reviews your deck plans, he or she will look for the following details. Make sure your plan drawings include this information when you visit the building inspection office to apply for a building permit.

- Overall size of the deck.
- Position of the deck relative to buildings and property lines. The deck must be set back at least 5 ft. from neighboring property.
- Location of all beams and posts.
- Size and on-center (OC) spacing of joists.
- Thickness of decking boards.
- Height of deck above the ground.
- Detailed drawings of joinery methods for all structural members of the deck.
- Type of soil that will support the concrete post footings: sand, gravel, or clay.
- Species of wood you will be using.
- Types of metal connectors and other hardware you plan to use when constructing your deck.

HOW TO
BUILD A DECK

Building Decks: A Step-by-step Overview

Deck-building is a project you'll tackle in stages, no matter what design you choose. Before you begin construction, review the photos on these two pages. They outline the basic procedure you'll want to follow when building your deck. The chapters to follow will explore each of these stages extensively.

Be sure to gather your tools and materials before you begin the project, and arrange to have a helper available for the more difficult stages. Check with local utilities for the location of underground electrical, telephone, or water lines before digging the footings. Apply for a building permit, where required, and make sure a building inspector has approved the deck design before beginning work.

The time it takes to build a deck depends on the size and complexity of the design as well as your building skills. If you're comfortable using tools and start with thorough, accurate plans, you should be able to complete a single-level deck in a few weekends.

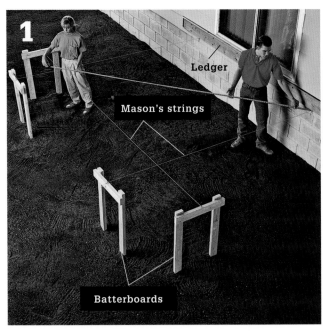

Install a ledger to anchor the deck to the house and to serve as reference for laying out footings (pages 38 to 45). Use batterboards and mason's strings to locate footings, and check for square by measuring diagonals (page 49).

Pour concrete post footings (pages 52 to 55), and install metal post anchors (pages 57 to 58). Set and brace the posts, attach them to the post anchors, and mark posts to show where beam will be attached (pages 58 to 61).

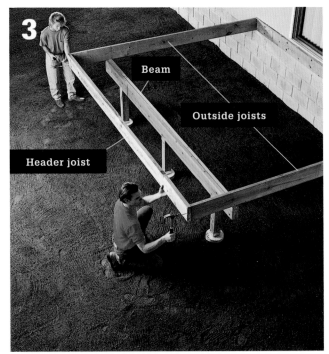

Fasten the beam to the posts (pages 62 to 65). Install the outside joists and header joist, using galvanized nails (pages 67 to 68).

Install metal joist hangers on the ledger and header joist, then hang the remaining joists (pages 68 to 71). Most decking patterns require joists that are spaced 16" on center.

Lay decking boards, and trim them with a circular saw (pages 104 to 117). If desired for appearance, cover pressure-treated header and outside joists with redwood or cedar facing boards (page 108).

Build deck stairs. Stairs provide access to the deck and establish traffic patterns.

Install a railing around the deck and stairway (page 140). A railing adds a decorative touch and may be required on any deck that is more than 30" above the ground. If desired, finish the underside of the deck (page 232).

Structural Support

Regardless of the deck design you choose, every deck has a fundamentally similar structure. Posts and footings anchored in the ground, working in tandem with a ledger board fastened to the house, support a framework of beams and joists that form a deck's undercarriage. Decking, railings, and steps are added to this platform to make it accessible and safe. There are proven techniques for installing each of these structural elements, and that's what you'll learn in this chapter. Once you get comfortable with these skills, you'll be able to apply them to any of the deck projects featured in this book—or create your own unique deck plans.

The end of the chapter will also show you important variations to basic techniques you may need to apply to your project, depending on the size, height or location of your new deck or the topography of your yard.

In this chapter:

- Installing a Ledger
- Locating Post Footings
- Digging & Pouring Footings
- Installing Posts
- Installing Beams
- Hanging Joists
- Framing Low-profile Decks
- Framing Multi-level Decks
- Framing Decks on Steep Slopes
- Working with Angles
- Creating Curves
- Framing for Insets

Installing a Ledger

The first step in building an attached deck is to fasten the ledger to the house. The ledger anchors the deck and establishes a reference point for building the deck square and level. The ledger also supports one end of all the deck joists, so it must be attached securely to the framing members of the house.

If your deck's ledger is made from pressure-treated lumber, make sure to use hot-dipped, galvanized lag screws and washers to attach it to the house. Ordinary zinc-coated hardware will corrode and eventually fail if placed in contact with ACQ pressure-treating chemicals.

Install the ledger so that the surface of the decking boards will be 1" below the indoor floor level. This height difference prevents rainwater or melted snow from seeping into the house.

Tools & Materials ▶

Pencil
Level
Circular saw with carbide blade
Chisel
Hammer
Metal snips
Caulk gun
Drill and bits
    (¼" twist, 1" spade, ⅜" and ⅝" masonry)
Ratchet wrench
Awl
Rubber mallet
Pressure-treated lumber
Galvanized flashing
8d galvanized common nails
Silicone caulk
⅜ × 4" lag screws and 1" washers
Lead masonry anchors for ⅜" lag screws
    (for brick walls)
2 × 4s for braces

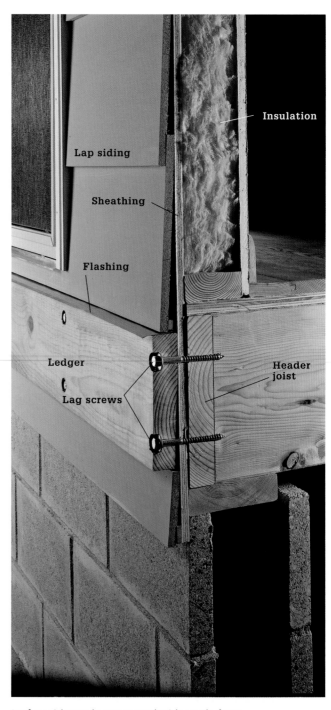

Ledger (shown in cross section) is made from pressure-treated lumber. Lap siding is cut away to expose sheathing and to provide a flat surface for attaching the ledger. Galvanized flashing tucked under siding prevents moisture damage to wood. Countersunk ⅜ × 4" lag screws hold ledger to header joist inside house. If there is access to the space behind the header joist, such as in an unfinished basement, attach the ledger with carriage bolts, washers, and nuts.

Labels on figure: Insulation, Lap siding, Sheathing, Flashing, Ledger, Lag screws, Header joist

How to Attach a Ledger to Lap Siding

1

Draw an outline showing where the deck will fit against the house, using a level as a guide. Include the thickness of the outside joists and any decorative facing boards that will be installed.

2

Cut out siding along outline, using a circular saw. Set blade depth to same thickness as siding, so that blade does not cut into sheathing.

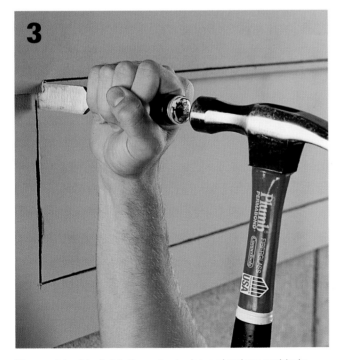

3

Use a chisel to finish the cutout where circular saw blade does not reach. Hold the chisel with the bevel-side in.

4

Measure and cut ledger from pressure-treated lumber. Remember that ledger will be shorter than overall length of cutout.

(continued)

5

Cut galvanized flashing to length of cutout, using metal snips. Slide flashing up under siding. Do not nail the metal flashing in place.

6

Center the ledger in the cutout, underneath the flashing. Brace in position, and tack ledger into place with 8d galvanized nails. Apply a thick bead of silicone caulk to crack between siding and flashing.

7

Drill pairs of ¼" pilot holes spaced every 2 feet, through the ledger and sheathing and into the header joist.

8

Counterbore each pilot hole to ½" depth, using a 1" spade bit.

Attach ledger to wall with ⅜ × 4" lag screws and washers, using a ratchet wrench or impact driver.

Seal lag screw heads with silicone caulk. Seal the crack between the wall and the sides and bottom of the ledger.

How to Attach a Ledger to Masonry

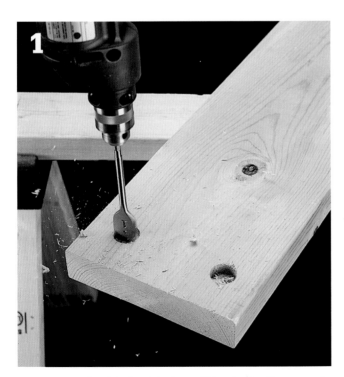

Measure and cut ledger. Ledger will be shorter than overall length of outline. Drill pairs of ¼" pilot holes every 2 feet in ledger. Counterbore each pilot hole to ½" depth, using a 1" spade bit.

Draw an outline of the deck on the wall, using a level as a guide. Center ledger in outline on wall, and brace in position. Mark the pilot hole locations on wall, using an awl or nail. Remove ledger.

(continued)

Drill anchor holes 3" deep into masonry, using a ⅝" masonry bit.

Drive lead masonry anchors for ⅜" lag screws into drilled holes, using a rubber mallet.

Attach ledger to wall with ⅜ × 4" lag screws and washers, using a ratchet wrench or impact driver. Tighten screws firmly, but do not overtighten.

Seal the cracks between the wall and ledger with silicone caulk. Also seal the lag screw heads.

How to Attach a Ledger to Stucco

Draw outline of deck on wall, using a level as a guide. Measure and cut ledger, and drill pilot holes (page 41, step 1). Brace ledger against wall, and mark hole locations, using a nail or awl.

Remove ledger. Drill pilot holes through stucco layer of wall, using a ⅜" masonry bit.

Extend each pilot hole through the sheathing and into the header joist, using a ¼" bit. Reposition ledger and brace in place.

Attach ledger to wall with ⅜ × 4" lag screws and washers, using a ratchet wrench. Seal the lag screw heads and the cracks between the wall and ledger with silicone caulk.

How to Attach a Ledger to Metal or Vinyl Siding

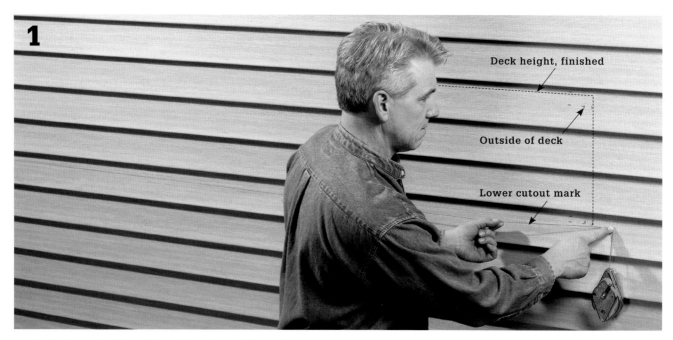

1

Deck height, finished

Outside of deck

Lower cutout mark

Mark the length of the ledger location, adding 1½" at each end to allow for the rim joists that will be installed later. Also allow for fascia board thickness if it will be added and create space for metal rim-joist hangers. Then mark the top and bottom edges of the ledger at both ends of its location. Snap lines for the ledger position between the marks. Check the lines for level and adjust as necessary. You may be able to use the siding edges to help determine the ledger location, but only after checking to see if the edges are level. Don't assume siding is installed level.

2

Set the circular saw blade depth to cut through the siding. Use a metal cutting blade for metal siding; a 40-tooth carbide blade works well on vinyl siding. Cut on the outside of the lines along the top and sides of the ledger location, stopping the blade when it reaches a corner.

3

Snap a new level line ½" above the bottom line and make your final cut along this line. This leaves a small lip of siding that will fit under the ledger.

4

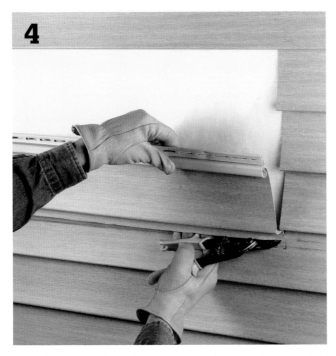

Complete the cuts in the corners, using tin snips on metal siding or a utility knife on vinyl siding. A hammer and sharp chisel also may be used.

5

Insert building felt underneath the siding and over the existing felt that has been damaged by the cuts. It is easiest to cut and install two long strips. Cut and insert the first strip so it is underneath the siding at the ends and bottom edge of the cutout and attach it with staples. Cut and insert the second strip so it is underneath the siding at the ends and top edge of the cutout, so that it overlaps the first strip by at least 3".

6

Cut and insert galvanized flashing (also called Z-flashing) underneath the full length of the top edge of the cutout. Do not use fasteners; pressure will hold the flashing in place until the ledger is installed.

7

Cut and install the ledger board (see pages 39 to 41).

Locating Post Footings

Establish the exact locations of all concrete footings by stretching mason's strings across the site. Use the ledger board as a starting point. These perpendicular layout strings will be used to locate holes for concrete footings and to position metal post anchors on the finished footings. Anchor the layout strings with temporary 2 × 4 supports, often called batterboards. You may want to leave the batterboards in place until after the footings are dug. That way, you can use the strings to accurately locate the J-bolts in the concrete.

Tools & Materials ▸

Tape measure	Line level
Felt-tipped pen	Plumb bob
Circular saw	2 × 4s
Screwgun	10d nails
Framing square	2½" wallboard screws
Masonry hammer	Mason's strings
Claw hammer	Masking tape

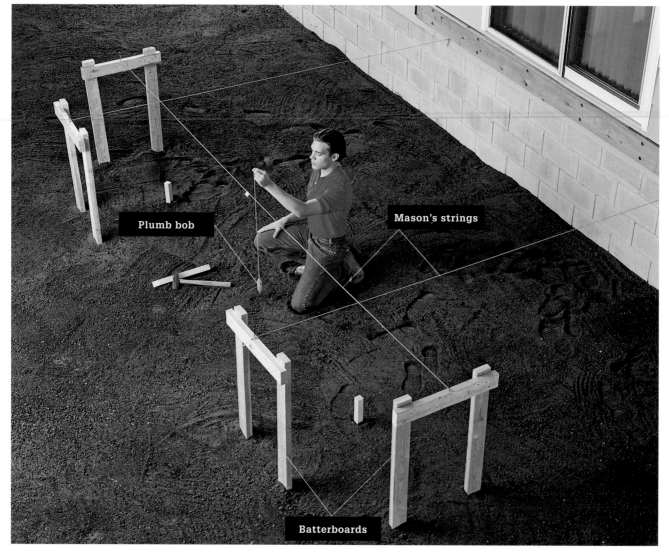

Mason's strings stretched between ledger and batterboards are used to position footings for deck posts. Use a plumb bob and stakes to mark the ground at the exact centerpoints of footings.

How to Locate Post Footings

1

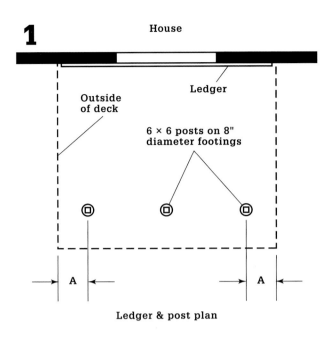

House

Ledger

Outside of deck

**6 × 6 posts on 8"
diameter footings**

A   A

Ledger & post plan

Use your design plan to find distance (A). Measure from the side of the deck to the center of each outside post. Use your elevation drawings to find the height of each deck post.

2

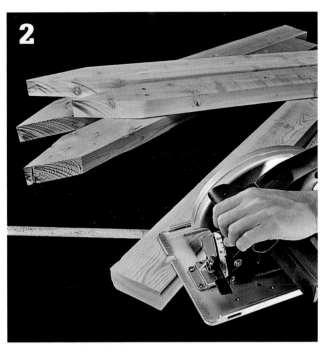

Cut 2 × 4 stakes for batterboards, each about 8" longer than post height. Trim one end of each stake to a point, using a circular saw. Cut 2 × 4 crosspieces, each about 2 feet long.

3

Assemble batterboards by attaching crosspieces to stakes with 2½" wallboard screws. Crosspieces should be about 2" below tops of stakes.

4

Transfer measurement A (step 1) to ledger, and mark reference points at each end of ledger. String lines will be stretched from these points on ledger.

(continued)

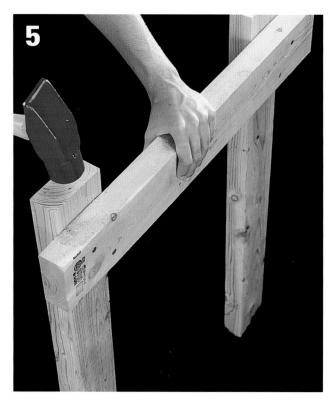

5

Drive a batterboard 6" into the ground, about 2 feet past the post location. Crosspiece of batterboard should be parallel to the ledger.

6

Drive a 10d nail into bottom of ledger at reference point (step 4). Attach a mason's string to nail.

7

Extend the mason's string so that it is taut and perpendicular to the ledger. Use a framing square as a guide. Secure the string temporarily by wrapping it several times around the batterboard.

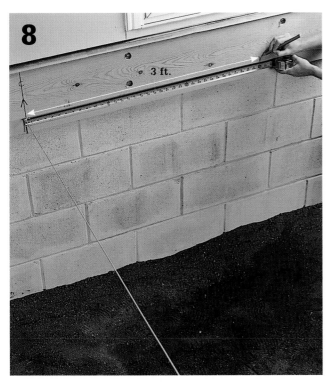

8

Check the mason's string for square using "3-4-5 carpenter's triangle." First, measure along the ledger 3 feet from the mason's string and mark a point, using a felt-tipped pen.

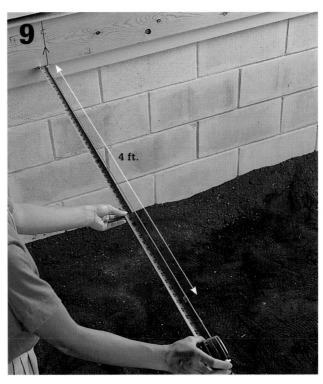

9

Measure mason's string 4 feet from edge of ledger, and mark with masking tape.

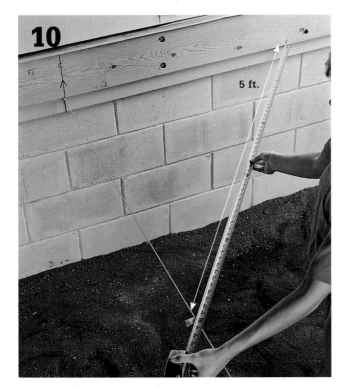

10

Measure distance between marks. If string is perpendicular to ledger, the distance will be exactly 5 feet. If necessary, move string left or right on batterboard until distance between marks is 5 feet.

11

Drive a 10d nail into top of batterboard at string location. Leave about 2" of nail exposed. Tie string to nail.

(continued)

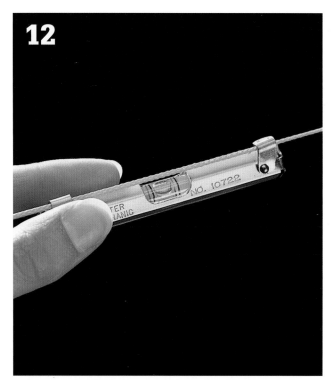

Hang a line level on the mason's string. Raise or lower string until it is level. Locate other outside post footing, repeating steps 5 to 12.

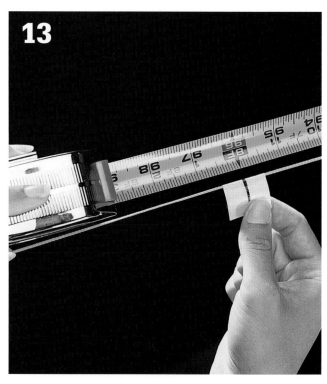

Measure along mason's strings from ledger to find centerpoint of posts. Mark centerpoints on strings, using masking tape.

Drive additional batterboards into ground, about 2 feet outside mason's strings and lined up with post centerpoint marks (step 13).

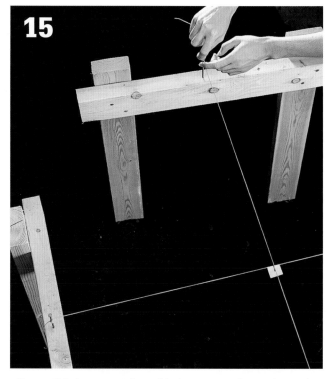

Align a third cross string with the centerpoint marks on the first strings. Drive 10d nails in new batterboards, and tie off cross string on nails. Cross string should be close to, but not touching, the first strings.

Check strings for square by measuring distances A-B and C-D. Measure diagonals A-D and B-C from edge of ledger to opposite corners. If strings are square, measurement A-B will be same as C-D, and diagonal A-D will be same as B-C. If necessary, adjust strings on batterboards until square.

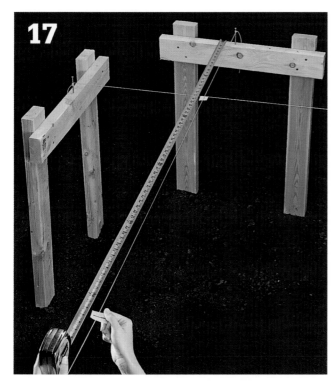

Measure along the cross string and mark centerpoints of any posts that will be installed between the outside posts.

Use a plumb bob to mark post centerpoints on the ground, directly under the marks on the mason's strings. Drive a stake into ground at each point. Remove mason's strings before digging footings.

Digging & Pouring Footings

Concrete footings hold deck posts in place and support the weight of the deck. Check local codes to determine the size and depth of footings required for your area. In cold climates, footings must be deeper than the soil frost line.

To help protect posts from water damage, each footing should be poured so that it is 2" above ground level. Tube-shaped forms let you extend the footings above ground level.

It is easy and inexpensive to mix your own concrete by combining portland cement, sand, gravel, and water.

As an alternative to inserting J-bolts into wet concrete, you can use masonry anchors, or install anchor bolts with an epoxy designed for deck footings and other masonry installations. The epoxy method provides you with more time to reset layout strings for locating bolt locations, and it eliminates the problem of J-bolts tilting or sinking into concrete that is too loose. Most building centers sell threaded rod, washers, nuts, and epoxy syringes, but you also can buy these items separately at most hardware centers.

Before digging, consult local utilities for location of any underground electrical, telephone, or water lines that might interfere with footings.

Power augers quickly dig holes for post footings. They are available at rental centers. Some models can be operated by one person, while others require two people (see page 203).

Tools & Materials ▸

Power auger
  or clamshell
  posthole digger
Tape measure
Pruning saw
Shovel
Reciprocating saw
  or handsaw
Torpedo level
Hoe
Trowel
Shovel
Old toothbrush
Plumb bob
Utility knife

Concrete tube forms
Portland cement
Sand
Gravel
J-bolts
Wheelbarrow
Scrap 2 × 4

How to Dig & Pour Post Footings

Dig holes for post footings with a clamshell digger or power auger, centering the holes on the layout stakes. For holes deeper than 35", use a power auger.

Measure hole depth. Local building codes specify depth of footings. Cut away tree roots, if necessary, using a pruning saw.

Pour 2" to 3" of loose gravel in the bottom of each footing hole. Gravel will provide drainage under concrete footings.

Add 2" to hole depth so that footings will be above ground level. Cut concrete tube forms to length, using a reciprocating saw or handsaw. Make sure cuts are straight.

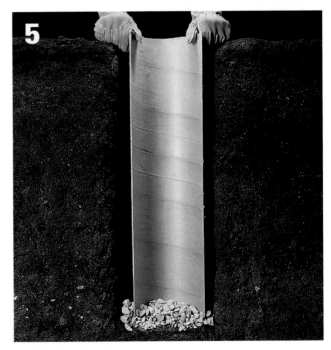

Insert tubes into footing holes, leaving about 2" of tube above ground level. Use a level to make sure tops of tubes are level. Pack soil around tubes to hold them in place.

(continued)

Mix dry ingredients for concrete in a wheelbarrow, using a hoe.

Form a hollow in center of dry concrete mixture. Slowly pour a small amount of water into hollow, and blend in dry mixture with a hoe.

Add more water gradually, mixing thoroughly until concrete is firm enough to hold its shape when sliced with a trowel.

Pour concrete slowly into the tube form, guiding concrete from the wheelbarrow with a shovel. Fill about half of the form, using a long stick to tamp the concrete, filling any air gaps in the footing. Then finish pouring and tamping concrete into the form.

Level the concrete by pulling a 2 × 4 across the top of the tube form, using a sawing motion. Add concrete to any low spots. Retie the mason's strings on the batterboards, and recheck measurements.

Insert a J-bolt at an angle into the wet concrete at center of the footing.

Lower the J-bolt slowly into the concrete, wiggling it slightly to eliminate any air gaps.

Set the J-bolt so ¾" to 1" is exposed above concrete. Brush away any wet concrete on bolt threads with an old toothbrush.

Use a plumb bob to make sure the J-bolt is positioned exactly at center of post location.

Use a torpedo level to make sure the J-bolt is plumb. If necessary, adjust the bolt and repack concrete. Let concrete cure, then cut away exposed portion of tube with a utility knife.

Installing Posts

Posts support the deck beams and transfer the weight of the deck, as well as everything on it, to the concrete footings. They create the above-ground foundation of your deck. Your building inspector will verify that the posts you plan to use are sized correctly to suit your deck design.

Choose post lumber carefully so the posts will be able to carry these substantial loads for the life of your deck. Pressure-treated lumber is your best defense against rot or insect damage. Select posts that are straight and free of deep cracks, large knots, or other natural defects that could compromise their strength. Try not to cut off the factory-treated ends when trimming the posts to length; they contain more of the treatment chemicals and generally last longer than cut ends. Face the factory ends down against the post hardware where water is more likely to accumulate.

Use galvanized metal post anchors to attach the posts to concrete footings. If posts are set directly on concrete, the ends won't dry properly. You'll also have a harder time making the necessary mechanical connection to the footings. Post anchors have drainage holes and pedestals that raise the ends of the wood above the footings and improve drainage. Make sure the posts are installed plumb for maximum strength.

Tools & Materials ▸

Pencil
Framing square
Ratchet wrench
Tape measure
Power miter saw or circular saw
Hammer
Screwgun
Level
Combination square
Metal post anchors
Nuts for J-bolts
Lumber for posts
6d galvanized common nails
2" wallboard screws
Long, straight 2 × 4
1 × 4s
Pointed 2 × 2 stakes

How to Attach Post Anchors

Mark the top of each footing as a reference line for installing post anchors. Lay a long, straight 2 × 4 flat across two or three concrete footings, parallel to the ledger, with one edge tight against the J-bolts.

Draw a reference line across each concrete footing, using an edge of the 2 × 4 as a guide. Remove the 2 × 4.

Place a metal post anchor on each concrete footing, and center it over the J-bolt.

(continued)

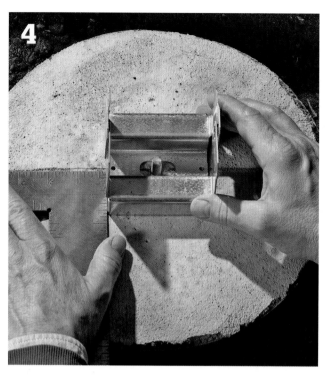

Use a framing square to make sure the post anchor is positioned square to the reference line drawn on the footing.

Thread a nut over each J-bolt, and tighten it securely with a ratchet wrench or impact driver.

How to Set Posts

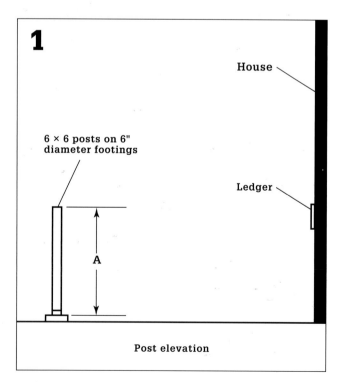

6 × 6 posts on 6" diameter footings

House

Ledger

A

Post elevation

Use the elevation drawing from your design plan to find the length of each post (A). Add 6" for a cutting margin.

Cut posts with power miter saw or circular saw. Make sure factory-treated ends of posts are square. If necessary, square them by trimming with a power miter saw or circular saw.

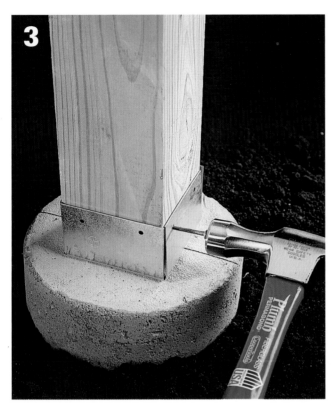

Place post in anchor, and tack into place with a single 6d galvanized common nail.

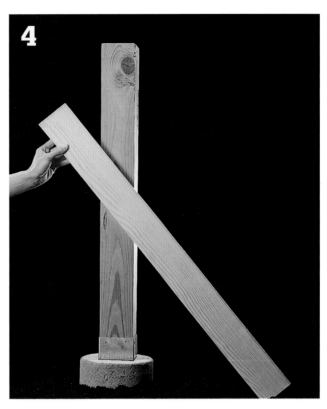

Brace post with a 1 × 4. Place the 1 × 4 flat across post so that it crosses the post at a 45° angle about halfway up.

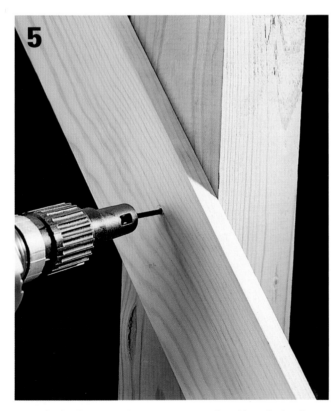

Attach the brace to the post temporarily with a single 2" wallboard screw.

Drive a pointed 2 × 2 stake into the ground next to the end of the brace.

(continued)

Use a level to make sure the post is plumb. Adjust the post, if necessary.

Attach the brace to the stake with two 2" wallboard screws.

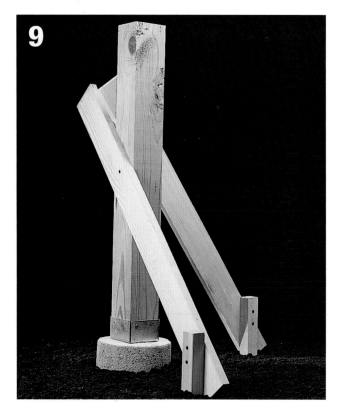

Plumb and brace the post on the side perpendicular to the first brace.

Attach the post to the post anchor with 6d galvanized common nails.

Position a straight 2 × 4 with one end on the ledger and the other end across the face of the post. Level the 2 × 4, then lower its post end ¼" for every 3 ft. between the ledger and the post (for water runoff). Draw a line on the post along the bottom of the 2 × 4. This line indicates the top of the joists.

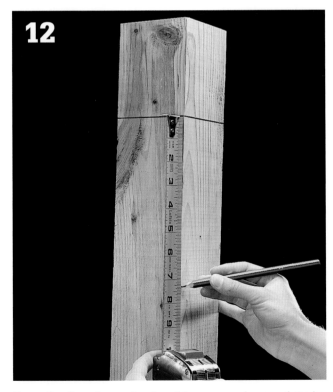

From the line shown in step 11, measure down and mark the posts a distance equal to the width of the joists.

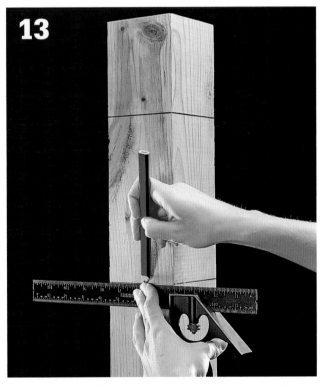

Use a square to draw a line completely around the post. This line indicates the top of the beam. From this line, repeat steps 12 and 13 to determine the bottom of the beam.

Installing Beams

Deck beams attach to the posts to help support the weight of the joists and decking. Installation methods depend on the deck design and local codes, so check with a building inspector to determine what is acceptable in your area.

In a saddle beam deck, the beam is attached directly on top of the posts. Metal fasteners, called post-saddles, are used to align and strengthen the beam-to-post connection. The advantage is that the post bears the weight of the deck.

A notched-post deck requires 6 × 6 posts notched at the post top to accommodate the full size of the beam. The deck's weight is transferred to the posts, as in a post-and-beam deck.

In years past, a third style of beam construction, called sandwiching, was also generally acceptable for deck construction. (You can see an example of it on p. 19.) It consisted of two beams that straddled both sides of the post, connected by long through bolts. Because this method has less strength than the saddle or notched styles, it is no longer approved by most building codes.

Tools & Materials ▸

Tape measure
Pencil
Circular saw
Paint brush
Combination square
Screwgun
Drill
⅜" auger bit
1" spade bit
Ratchet wrench
Caulk gun
Reciprocating saw or handsaw
Pressure-treated lumber
Clear sealer-preservative
2½" galvanized deck screws
10d joist hanger nails
⅜ × 8" carriage bolts with washers and nuts
⅜ × 2" lag screws
Silicone caulk

Deck beams, resting in a notch on the tops of the posts and secured with through bolts and nuts, guarantee strong connections that will bear the weight of your deck.

How to Fabricate a Beam

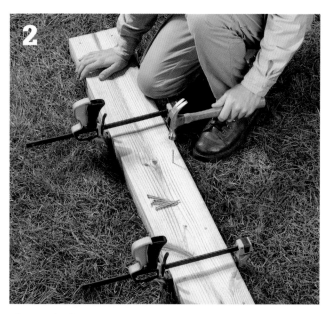

Select two straight boards of the same dimension (generally 2 × 8 or larger) and lay them face to face to see which alignment comes closest to flush on all sides. Apply exterior grade construction adhesive to one board and lay the mating board onto it. Drive a pair of 10d nails near the end of the assembly to pin the boards together.

Clamp the beam members together every two or three feet, forcing the boards into alignment as you go, if necessary. Drive 10d nails in a regular, staggered pattern every 12" to 16" or so. Flip the beam over and repeat the nailing pattern from the other side.

How to Mark Post Locations on a Beam

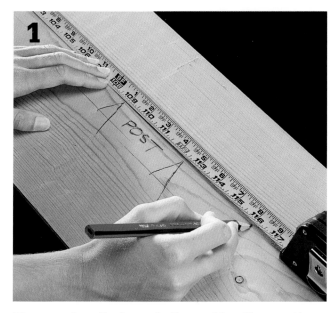

Measure along the beam to the post locations, making sure the ends of the boards of a doubled beam are flush. Mark both the near and far edges of the post onto the beam.

Use a combination square or speed square to transfer the post marks onto the top and then the other face of the beam, allowing you to make sure the post and post hardware align with both faces.

How to Install a Beam with a Post Saddle

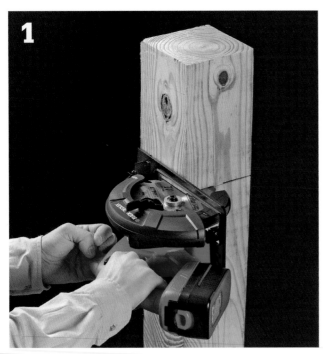

Cut the post to final height after securing it in place. Make two passes with a circular saw or one pass with a reciprocating saw. For most DIYers, the circular saw option will yield a more even cut.

Attach the saddle hardware to the top of the post using joist hanger screws, 10d galvanized common nails, or joist hanger nails. You must drive a fastener at every predrilled hole in the saddle hardware.

Set the beam into the saddle, making sure the sides of the saddle align with the layout marks on the beam.

Secure the beam into the saddle by driving galvanized common nails or joist hanger screws through the predrilled holes in the top half of the saddle.

How to Install a Beam for a Notched-post Deck

Remove 6 × 6 posts from post anchors and cut to finished height. Measure and mark a notch at the top of each post, sized to fit the thickness and width of the beam. Trace the lines on all sides using a framing square.

Use a circular saw to rough-cut the notches, then switch to a reciprocating saw or hand saw to finish. Reattach posts to the post anchors, with the notch-side facing away from the deck.

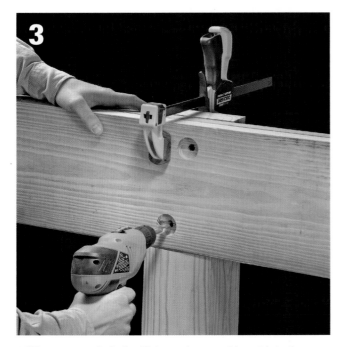

With someone's help, lift beam (crown side up) into the notches. Align beam and clamp to posts. Counterbore two ½"-deep holes, using a 1" spade bit, then drill ⅜" pilot holes through the beam and post, using a ⅜" auger bit.

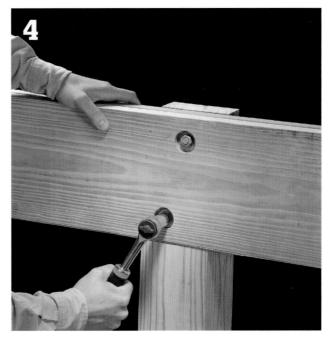

Insert carriage bolts to each pilot hole. Add a washer and nut to the counterbore-side of each, and tighten using a ratchet. Seal both ends with silicone caulk. Apply self-sealing membrane to top surfaces of beam and posts if necessary (see page 200).

Hanging Joists

Joists provide support for the decking boards. They are attached to the ledger and header joist with galvanized metal joist hangers and are nailed to the top of the beam.

For strength and durability, use pressure-treated lumber for all joists. The exposed outside joists and header joist can be faced with redwood or cedar boards for a more attractive appearance.

Tools & Materials ▸

Tape measure	Drill	10d and 16d	Galvanized metal
Pencil	Twist bits (1/16", 1/4")	galvanized	joist hangers
Hammer	1" spade bit	common nails	3/8 × 4" lag screws
Combination square	Pressure-treated	Clear sealer-	and 1" washers
Circular saw	lumber	preservative	
Paintbrush	10d joist hanger nails	Joist angle brackets	

Metal joist hangers attached to rim joists or ledgers are practically foolproof for hanging intermediate deck joists. Look for hanger hardware that is triple-dipped galvanized metal.

How to Hang Joists

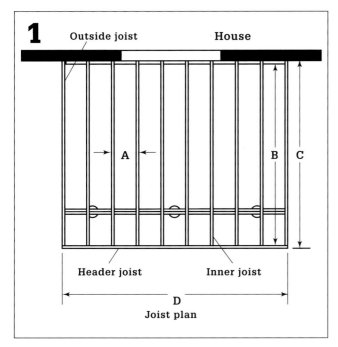

Use your deck plan to find the spacing (A) between joists, and the length of inner joists (B), outside joists (C), and header joist (D). Measure and mark lumber for outside joists, using a combination square as a guide. Cut joists with a circular saw. Seal cut ends with clear sealer-preservative.

Attach joist hanger hardware near each end of the ledger board, according to your layout. Previous building codes allowed you to face nail the joists into the ends of the ledger, but this is no longer accepted practice. Attach only enough fasteners to hold the hanger in position while you square up the joist layout.

Attach the outside joists to the top of the beam by toenailing them with 10d galvanized common nails.

Trim off the ends of structural lumber to get a clean straight edge.

(continued)

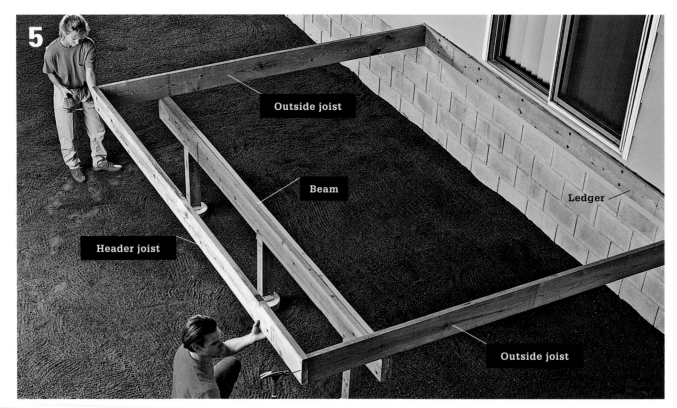

5

Outside joist

Beam

Ledger

Header joist

Outside joist

Measure and cut header joist. Seal cut ends with clear sealer-preservative. Drill ¹⁄₁₆" pilot holes at each end of header joist. Attach header to ends of outside joists with 16d galvanized common nails. For extra reinforcement, you can add metal corner brackets to the inside corner joints.

6

Finish nailing the end joist hangers, making sure you have a joist hanger nail in every punched hole in the hanger.

7

Measure along ledger from edge of outside joist, and mark where joists will be attached to ledger.

Draw the outline of each joist on the ledger, using a combination square as a guide.

Measure along the beam from outside joist, and mark where joists will cross the beam. Draw the outlines across top of both beam boards.

Measure along the header joist from the outside joist, and mark where joists will be attached to header joist. Draw the outlines on the inside of the header, using a combination square as a guide.

Attach joist hangers to the ledger and to the header joist. Position each hanger so that one of the flanges is against the joist outline. Nail one flange to framing members with 10d galvanized common nails.

(continued)

12

Cut a scrap board to use as a spacer. Hold spacer inside each joist hanger, then close the hanger around the spacer.

13

Nail the remaining side flange to the framing member with 10d joist hanger nails. Remove spacer.

14

Measure and mark lumber for joists, using a combination square as a guide. Cut joists with a circular saw or power miter saw.

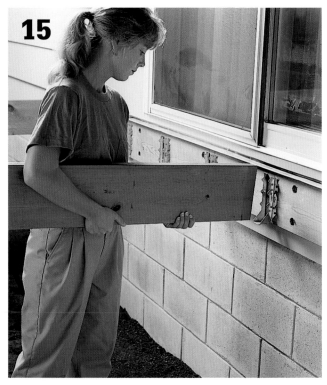

15

Seal cut ends with clear sealer-preservative. Place joists in hangers with crowned edge up.

Attach the ledger joist hangers to the joists with joist hanger nails. Drive nails into both sides of each joist.

Align the joists with the outlines drawn on the top of the beam. Anchor the joists to the beam by toenailing from both sides with 10d galvanized nails.

Alternate Method ▶

Fasten joists to beams using H-fit joist ties for strength and durability.

Attach the joists to the hangers on the joist with 10d joist hanger nails. Drive nails into both sides of each joist.

Framing Low-profile Decks

Building a deck that sits very close to the ground generally is easier than constructing a very high deck, but low-profile situations do require some design modifications. If the deck is extremely low (8" to 12" high), it is best to rest the beams directly on the concrete footings, since posts are not practical. The joists usually are hung on the faces of the beams rather than resting on top of the beams; cantilever designs are rarely used. Since the ledger is mounted so low on the house, it may need to be anchored to the foundation wall rather than to the rim joist (right).

A deck that is more than 12" above the ground should have at least one step, either box-frame style, or suspended from the deck.

Masonry sleeves are used to attach a ledger to a masonry foundation. Drill 3"-deep guide holes for the sleeves, using a ⅝" masonry bit, then drive sleeves for ⅜"-diameter lag screws into the holes. Position the ledger, then attach it with lag screws driven through the ledgers and into the masonry sleeves.

Beams for a low-profile deck often rest directly on concrete footings, with no posts. Because low-profile decks may require 2 × 8 or 2 × 6 joists, an intermediate beam may be required to provide adequate support for these narrower joists. At each end of the last beam, the outside timber must be 1½" longer than the inside timber, creating a recess where the end of the rim joist will fit.

How to Install Low-profile Beams & Joists

Install the ledger, then lay out and dig footings. If beams will rest directly on footings, use tube forms. Raise the tubes to the proper height and check them for plumb as you pour the concrete. Smooth off the surfaces of the footings, and insert direct-bearing hardware while the concrete is still wet, using layout strings to ensure that the hardware is aligned correctly.

Construct beams (page 63), then set the beams into the direct-bearing hardware. Drill pilot holes and use 3½" lag bolts to secure the beam to the hardware. Mark joist locations on the faces of the beams, then install joist hangers.

Cut and install all joists, attaching them with joist-hanger nails. Complete your deck, using standard deck-building techniques. Install a box-frame or suspended step, if desired (see page 123).

Framing Multi-level Decks

A multi-level deck has obvious advantages, but many do-it-yourselfers are wary of building such a deck, feeling that it is too complex. In reality, however, a multi-level deck is nothing more than two or more adjacent deck platforms set at different heights. You can build a multi-level deck with the same simple construction techniques used to build a standard deck—with one exception: For efficiency, multi-level decks usually are designed so the platforms share a single support beam on the side where they meet. For this reason, it is essential that the shared posts and beams be sturdy enough to carry the load of both platforms.

Except for the shared beam, the separate platforms on a multi-level deck are independent and can use different construction methods. For example, the upper level might use a post and beam design with decking boards installed perpendicular to the joists, while the lower level might use a curved cantilever design with decking laid at an angle. If your time and budget are limited, you can build your deck in phases, completing one platform at a time, at your convenience.

Remember to include railings and stairs where needed. Any deck platform more than 30" above the ground—or above a lower deck platform—requires a railing.

Creating structural support in a multi-level deck requires a bit of ingenuity and planning. For example, a sturdy support wall may be constructed on a lower deck to support an upper, as above. Note that new codes do not allow you to attach beams by mounting them to the sides of posts, even if you use metal hanger hardware.

Multi-level Support Options

The shared beam method has one beam supporting both platforms where they overlap. The upper platform rests directly on the beam, while the lower hangs from the face of the beam. This method is an economical choice, since only one beam is required, and it is well suited for relatively flat building sites where the deck levels are close together. See pages 76 to 77.

The support-wall method features a top platform supported by a stud wall that rests on the lower platform, directly over the beam and posts. Unlike the methods listed above, the support-wall method requires that the lower deck platform be built first. This method is a good choice when you want to use decorative wall materials, such as cedar siding, to cover the gap between the two platforms. The support-wall method also works well if you want to complete your deck in phases, delaying construction of the upper level. See pages 78 to 79.

How to Install Shared Beam Support

Joist location

Beam location

Final cut-off

After laying out and installing the ledger and all posts and footings, mark the posts to indicate where the beam will rest. Use a straight 2 × 4 and a level to establish a point that is level with the top of the ledger, then measure down a distance equal to the height of the joists plus the height of the beam. Cut off the posts at this point, using a reciprocating saw.

Position a post-beam cap on each post. Construct a beam from 2 × 10 or 2 × 12 dimension lumber (page 63), then position the beam in the post-beam caps. If the beam is crowned, install it so the crowned side is up; if there is a gap between the middle cap and the beam, shim under the gap. Secure the post-beam caps to the posts and beam with galvanized deck screws.

Lay out joist locations for the upper platform on the ledger and on the top of the beam, then use a carpenter's square to transfer joist marks for the lower platform onto the face of the beam. Attach joist hangers at the joist layout lines on the ledger.

Measure, cut, and install joists for the upper platform, leaving a 1½" setback to allow for the thickness of the rim joist. At the beam, secure the joists by toenailing with 16d galvanized nails.

Attach joist hangers for the lower platform along the face of the beam, using a scrap piece of lumber as a spacer. Cut and install the joists for the lower platform.

Cut rim joists for both the upper and lower platforms, and attach them to the ends of the joists by endnailing with 16d nails. Complete the deck, using standard deck-building techniques.

How to Install a Deck Support Wall

Lay out and install the ledger and all posts and footings, then frame the lower platform, using standard deck-building techniques.

Use a straight 2 × 4 and a level to establish a reference point level with the bottom of the ledger, then find the total height for the support wall by measuring the vertical distance to the top of the lower platform. Cut the wall studs 3" less than this total height, to allow for the thickness of the top and bottom plates.

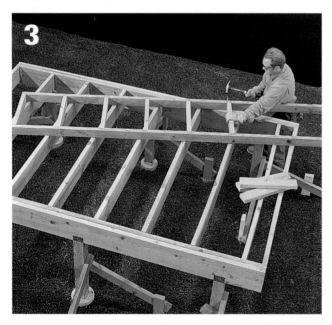

Cut 2 × 4 top and bottom plates to cover the full width of the upper platform, then lay out the stud locations on the plates, 16" on center. Cut studs to length, then assemble the support wall by endnailing the plates to the studs, using galvanized 16d nails.

Set a long "sway" brace diagonally across the stud wall, and nail it near one corner only. Square the wall by measuring the diagonals and adjusting until both diagonal measurements are the same. When the wall is square, nail the brace at the other corner, and to each stud. Cut off the ends of the brace flush with the plates.

5

Raise the support wall into position, aligning it with the edge of the beam and the end of the deck. Nail the sole plate to the beam with 16d galvanized nails driven on both sides of each stud.

6

Adjust the wall so it is plumb, then brace it in position by nailing a 1 × 4 across the end stud and outside joist.

7

Lay out joist locations for the upper platform, and install joist hangers on the ledger. Cut joists so they are 1½" shorter than the distance from the ledger to the front edge of the wall. Install the joists by toenailing them to the top plate with 16d nails. Remove the braces.

8

Measure and cut a rim joist, and attach it to the ends of the joists by endnailing with 16d nails. Also toenail the rim joist to the top plate of the support wall. Complete the deck, using standard deck-building techniques.

Framing Decks on Steep Slopes

Constructing a deck on a steep slope can be a complicated job if you use standard deck-building techniques. Establishing a layout for posts and footings is difficult on steeply pitched terrain, and construction can be demanding when one end of the deck is far above your head.

Professional deck contractors adapt to steep slope situations by using a temporary post-and-beam support structure, and by slightly altering the construction sequence. Rather than beginning with post-footing layout, experienced builders begin by constructing the outer frame and raising it onto a temporary support structure. Once the elevated frame is in position, the locations of the permanent posts and footings can be determined.

In most instances, you will need helpers when building a deck on a steep slope. To raise and position the deck frame on temporary supports, for example, you will need the help of three or four other people. *Note: The steep slope deck construction shown on the following pages was built using primarily 4 × 4" posts. Recent changes to some building codes indicate a preference for 6 × 6" posts. Always check with your local building department to learn applicable codes for your deck.*

Another important consideration when building a deck on a steep slope is the composition of the soil. The slope needs to be stable and suitable for anchoring deep footings. If the earth is loose, rocky or prone to erosion, have it inspected by a landscape architect or civil engineer first to make sure it will safely support a deck. The slope may need to be stabilized in other ways before construction begins.

If building the deck will require working at heights, use temporary support ledgers and bracing to prevent falls from ladders. Consider installing scaffolding, which may be a better solution than ladders if several people will be assisting you with the project. Scaffolding is available at many large rental centers for reasonable weekly and monthly rates.

The directions on the following pages show the construction of a deck featuring a corner-post design, but the technique can easily be adapted to canti-levered decks.

Positioning and measuring posts on a steep slope is much easier if the deck frame is already in position, resting on temporary supports.

Building Decks on Slopes

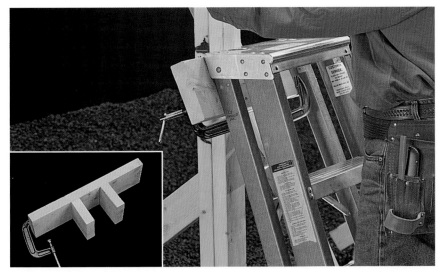

Stepladders should be used in the open position only if the ground is level. On uneven ground you can use a closed stepladder by building a support ledger from 2 × 6 scraps (inset) and clamping it to a post. Lean the closed ladder against the ledger, and level the base of the ladder, if necessary (below). Never climb onto the top step of the ladder.

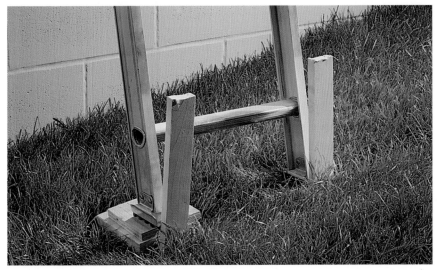

Extension ladders should be leveled and braced. Install sturdy blocking under ladder legs if the ground is uneven or soft, and drive a stake behind each ladder foot to keep it from slipping. Never exceed the weight limit printed on the ladder.

Scaffolding can be rented from rental centers or paint supply stores. When working at heights, scaffolding offers a safer, more stable working surface. Place blocking under the legs of the scaffolding, and level it by screwing the threaded legs in or out.

How to Build a Deck on a Steep Slope

After installing the ledger, use spray paint or stakes to mark the approximate locations for the post footings, according to your deck plans. Lay two 2 × 12 scraps on the ground to support temporary posts. Level the scraps, and anchor them with stakes. The bases for the temporary posts should be at least 2 ft. away from post-footing locations.

Construct two temporary posts by facenailing pairs of long 2 × 4s together. Erect each post by positioning it on the base and attaching a diagonal 2 × 4 brace. Toenail the post to the base.

Attach a second diagonal brace to each post, running at right angles to the first brace. Adjust the posts until they are plumb, then secure them in place by driving stakes into the ground and screwing the diagonal braces to the stakes.

Mark a cutoff line on each post by holding a long, straight 2 × 4 against the bottom of the ledger and the face of the post, then marking the post along the bottom edge of the 2 × 4. Cut off the posts at this height, using a reciprocating saw.

Construct a temporary support beam at least 2 ft. longer than the width of your deck by facenailing a pair of 2 × 4s together. Center the beam on top of the posts, and toenail it in place.

Build the outer frame of your deck according to your construction plans, and attach joist hangers to the inside of the frame, spaced 16" on center. With several helpers, lift the frame onto the temporary supports and carefully move it into position against the ledger. *Note: On very large or high decks, you may need to build the frame piece-by-piece on top of the temporary supports.*

(continued)

Endnail the side joists to the ends of the ledger, then reinforce the joint by installing angle brackets in the inside corners of the frame.

Check to make sure the frame is square by measuring the diagonals. If the measurements are not the same, adjust the frame on the temporary beam until it is square. Also check the frame to make sure it is level; if necessary, shim between the temporary beam and the side joists to level the frame. Toenail the frame to the temporary beam.

Use a plumb bob suspended from the deck frame to stake the exact locations for post footings on the ground. *Note: Make sure the footing stakes correspond to the exact center of the posts, as indicated by your deck plans.*

Dig and pour footings for each post. While the concrete is still wet, insert J-bolts for post anchors, using a plumb bob to ensure that the bolts are at the exact center of the post locations. Let the concrete dry completely before continuing.

Check once more to make sure the deck frame is square and level, and adjust if necessary. Attach post anchors to the footings, then measure from the anchors to the bottom edge of the deck beam to determine the length for each post. *Note: If your deck uses a cantilever design, make sure to allow for the height of the beam when cutting the posts.*

Cut posts and attach them to the beam and footing with post-beam caps and post anchors. Brace the posts by attaching 2 × 4 boards diagonally from the bottom of the post to the inside surface of the deck frame. Remove the temporary supports, then complete the project using standard deck-building techniques.

Working with Angles

Decks with geometric shapes and angled sides have much more visual interest than basic square or rectangular decks. Most homes and yards are configured with predictable 90° angles and straight sides, so an angled deck offers a pleasing visual surprise.

Contrary to popular belief, elaborate angled decks are relatively easy to plan and build, if you follow the lead of professional designers. As professionals know, most polygon-shaped decks are nothing more than basic square or rectangular shapes with one or more corners removed. An octagonal island deck, for example, is simply a square with all four corners omitted.

Seen in this light, complicated multi-level decks with many sides become easier to visualize and design.

For visual balance and ease of construction, use 45° angles when designing an angled, geometric deck. In this way, the joinery requires only common cutting angles (90°, 45°, or 22½°), and you can use skewed 45° joist hangers, readily available at home centers. *Note: The angled deck construction shown on the following pages was built using primarily 4 × 4" posts. Recent changes to some building codes indicate a preference for 6 × 6" posts. Always check with your local building department to learn applicable codes for your deck.*

Joists on a cantilevered deck can be easily marked for angled cuts by snapping a chalk line between two points on adjacent sides of the deck corner. Marking and cutting joists in this fashion is easier than measuring and cutting the joists individually. To help hold the joists in place while marking, tack a brace across the ends. Mark joist locations on the brace for reference.

Design Options for Angled Decks

Cantilever design is the easiest and least expensive to build, since it requires the fewest posts. But the length of the angled side is limited by code regulations that restrict the amount of joist overhang. And since the joists rest on top of the beam, cantilever designs are not suited for a deck with a very low profile. On cantilever designs, the joists along the angled side are beveled at 45° at the ends and are attached to the rim joist by endnailing.

Corner-post design is a good choice for large decks with long angled sides. It also works well for low-profile decks, since the joists are mounted to the inside faces of the beams. Many builders use a single beveled post to support the angled corners on this type of deck, but our method calls for two posts and footings at each of these corners, making the design easier to construct and more versatile. On a corner-post deck, the joists on the angled side are square-cut, and are attached to the beam with skewed 45° joist hangers (see page 43).

Multi-level design features an upper platform built using the corner-post method (above), but adds a lower platform. The lower level is supported by a second angled beam, created by sandwiching timbers around the same posts that support the upper platform. On the lower platform, the joists rest on top of the beam and are beveled on the back ends so they are flush with the edge of the beam. Check with your local building department to make sure this design strategy is still allowed.

Design & Construction of Angled Decks

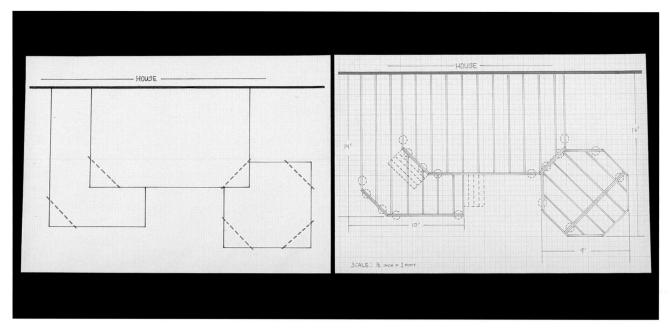

Draw squares and rectangles to create the basic deck platforms, then form angles by eliminating one or more corners. Using this method, you can design an almost infinite variety of single- and multi-level geometric decks. To ensure 45° angles, make sure the sides of the removed corners are the same length.

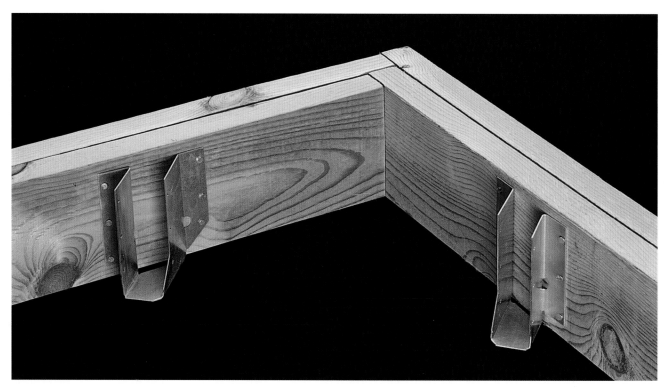

Use skewed 45° joist hangers to install joists when the beams are not parallel to the ledger. When mounted with skewed hangers, joists can be square-cut at the ends. Skewed 45° joist hangers are available at building centers in both left- and right-hand skews. However, if your deck joists angle away from the beam at angles other than 45°, you will need to special order skewed joist hangers to fit your situation, or use skewable joist hangers (page 196).

How to Build Support for an Angled Deck

Lay out and begin construction, using standard deck-building techniques. After installing the joists, mark cutting lines on the angled side by snapping a chalk line across the tops of the joists. Make sure the chalk line is angled 45° to the edge of the deck.

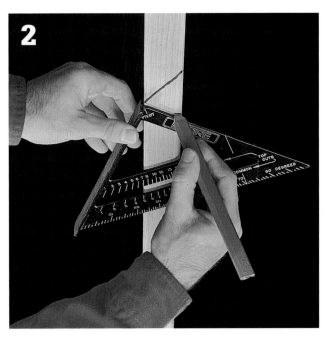

At the outside joists, use a speed square to change the 45° chalk line to a line angled at 22½° in the opposite direction. When joined to a rim joist that is also cut to 22½°, the corner will form the correct angle.

Use a combination square to extend the angle marks down the faces of the joists. Bevel-cut the deck joists with a circular saw, using a clamped board as a guide for the saw foot. Interior joists should be beveled to 45°; outside joists to 22½°.

Cut and install the rim joists. At the angled corners, bevel-cut the ends of the rim joists at 22½°. Endnail the rim joists in place, and reinforce the inside corners with adjustable angle brackets attached with joist-hanger nails. Finish the deck, using standard deck-building techniques.

How to Build an Angled Deck Using the Corner-post Design

Use boards to create a rectangular template of the deck. To ensure that the template is square, use the 3-4-5 triangle method: From the corner directly below the ledger, measure 3 ft. along the foundation, and mark a point. Measure out along the template board 4 ft., and mark a second point. Measure diagonally between the two points. This measurement should be 5 ft.; if not, adjust the template to square it.

Indicate each angled edge by positioning a board diagonally across the corner of the template. To ensure that the angles measure 45°, make sure the perpendicular legs of the triangle have exactly the same measurement. Nail the boards together where they overlap.

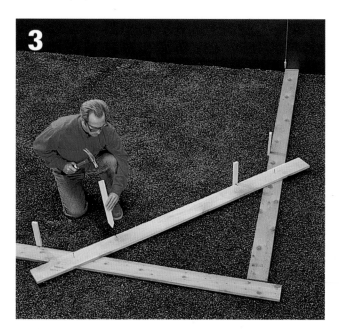

Mark locations for post footings with stakes or spray paint. At each 45° corner, mark locations for two posts, positioned about 1 ft. on each side of the corner. Temporarily move the board template, then dig and pour concrete footings.

While the concrete is still wet, reposition the template and check to make sure it is square to the ledger. Use a nail to scratch a reference line across the concrete next to the template boards, then insert J-bolts in the wet concrete. Let the concrete dry completely.

Attach metal post anchors to the J-bolts, centering them on the reference lines scratched in the concrete. The front and back edges of the anchors should be parallel to the reference line.

Measure and cut beam timbers to size. On ends that will form angled corners, use a speed square to mark 22½° angles on the tops of the timbers, then use a combination square to extend cutting lines down the face of the boards. Use a circular saw set for a 22½° bevel to cut off the timbers, then join them together with 16d nails.

Set posts into the post anchors, then use a mason's string and line level to mark cutoff lines on the posts at a point level with the bottom of the ledger. Cut off the posts, using a reciprocating saw. Attach post-beam caps to the posts, then set the beams into place. Secure beam corners together with adjustable angle brackets attached to the inside of each corner with joist-hanger nails.

(continued)

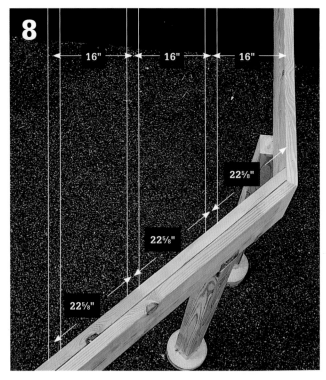

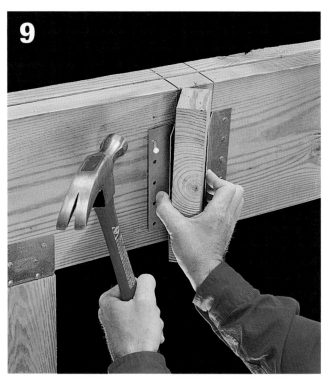

Measure and mark joist locations on the ledger and beams. If your joists are spaced 16" on center along the ledger, they will be spaced 22⅝" apart measured along the angled beam. If they are spaced 24" on center at the ledger, the joists will be spaced 33⁵⁄₁₆" apart along the angled beam.

Attach joist hangers at the layout marks on the ledger and beam. Use skewed 45° joist hangers on the angled beam.

Cut and install joists, securing them with joist-hanger nails. Joists installed in skewed 45° joist hangers can be square-cut; they need not be beveled to match the angle of the beam. Complete the deck, using standard deck-building techniques.

Corner-post Variation: Adding a Second Platform

After installing the beam and joists for the top deck platform, mark the posts to indicate where the beam for the lower platform will be attached. Remember that the joists for the lower deck platform will rest on top of the beam. To help measure for beam length, clamp scrap pieces of 2 × 4 to the front and back faces of the posts over the layout marks. At corners, the ends of the 2 × 4s should touch.

Determine the length for each beam timber by measuring from the point where the 2 × 4 blocks touch. Remember that this measurement represents the short side of the bevel-cut timbers.

Lay out and cut beam timbers to length. At angled ends, cut the timbers with a 22½° bevel. Position and attach the beams to the posts, using 3" lag screws and joist ties. Reinforce angled corners with adjustable angle brackets attached with joist-hanger nails (photo, step 4). Install the remaining posts for the lower platform.

Measure and cut joists for the lower platform, attaching them to the beam by toenailing with 16d nails. Where joists rest on the angled beam, position the joists so they overhang the beam, then scribe cutting lines along the back edge of the beam. Bevel-cut the joists to this angle. Cut and install rim joists, then complete the deck, using standard deck-building techniques.

Creating Curves

By their nature, curved shapes lend a feeling of tranquility to a landscape. A deck with curved sides tends to encourage quiet relaxation. A curved deck can also provide an effective visual transition between the sharp architectural angles of the house and the more sweeping natural lines of the surrounding landscape.

Curved decks nearly always use a cantilevered design (page 24), in which the curved portion of the deck overhangs a beam that is set back from the edge of the deck. This setback distance generally should be no more than one-third of the total length of the deck joists, but longer cantilevers are possible if you use a combination of thicker joists, closer joist spacing, and stronger wood species, such as southern yellow pine.

Note: The curved deck shown on the following pages was built using primarily 4 × 4" posts. Recent changes to some building codes indicate a preference for 6 × 6" posts. Always check with your local building department to learn applicable codes for your deck.

If your curved deck will be high enough to require a railing, we recommend a design that incorporates a circular curve rather than an elliptical or irregular curve. Adding a curved railing (pages 157 to 159) is much easier if the deck curve is based on a circular shape.

A curved deck is created by cutting joists to match the curved profile, then attaching a curved rim joist, which can be shaped in one of two ways (page opposite). Braces attached to the tops of the joists hold them in place as the rim joist is installed.

Curves and Deck Design ▸

Adding curves to your deck is not something you should do on the spur of the moment. Consider the pros and cons carefully before you commit to curves. Here are some to think about:

Pros:
- Curves can add visual appeal and uniqueness to your deck.
- Curves soften the overall feeling.
- Used wisely, curves have a natural, organic visual quality.
- A curve can be used to work around an obstacle in a pleasing way.
- A curved corner can preserve space below the deck.

Cons:
- Decks that incorporate curves almost always require more posts and beams, and they make less efficient use of building materials.
- A deck with curves takes at least twice as long to build as a square or rectangular one.
- Curved railings are tricky to make.
- Impact is lessened if curves are overused.
- Curves reduce and constrict deck floorspace.

Design Options for Curved Decks

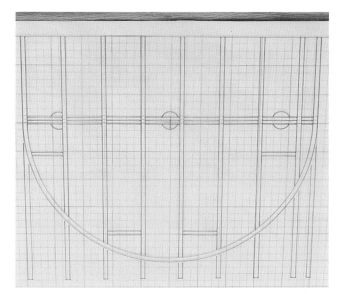

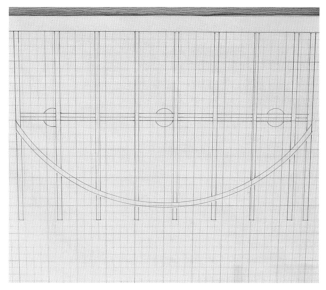

Circular designs are the best choice for curved decks that require railings. However, circular curves require a fairly long cantilever, a limitation that may limit the overall size of your deck. Circular decks are laid out using simple geometry and a long compass tool, called a trammel, which you can make yourself.

Irregular or elliptical curves should be used only on relatively low decks, since railings are quite difficult to construct for this kind of curve. These designs also work well for large decks, since the amount of overhang on the cantilever is relatively short compared to that for a circular curve.

Construction Options

Kerfed rim joist is formed by making a series of thin vertical cuts (kerfs) across the inside face of the board, making it flexible enough to wrap around the curve. A kerfed rim joist made from 2"-thick dimension lumber is sufficiently strong, but if you are kerfing a 1"-thick redwood or cedar fascia board, it should be backed with a laminated rim joist (photo, right).

Laminated rim joist is made by bending several layers of flexible ¼"- or ⅜"-thick exterior-grade plywood around the curve, joining each layer to the preceding layer with glue and screws. A laminated rim joist can stand alone, or it can provide backing for a more decorative fascia, such as a kerfed redwood or cedar board.

How to Lay Out a Curved Deck

Install posts and beam for a cantilivered deck. Cut joists slightly longer than their final length, and attach them to the ledger and the beam. Add cross-blocking between the two outside joists to ensure that they remain plumb.

Mark the joist spacing on a 1 × 4 brace, and tack it across the tops of the joists at the point where the deck curve will begin. Measure the distance between the inside edges of the outer joists at each end of the beam, then divide this measurement in half to determine the radius of the circular curve. Mark the 1 × 4 brace to indicate the midpoint of the curve.

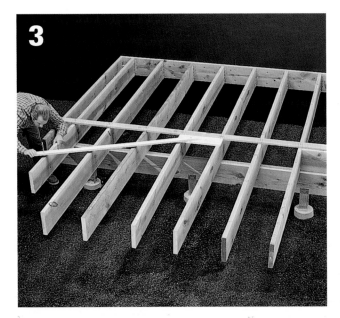

Build a trammel by anchoring one end of a long, straight 1 × 2 to the centerpoint of the curve, using a nail. (If the centerpoint lies between joists, attach a 1 × 4 brace across the joists to provide an anchor.) Measure out along the arm of the trammel a distance equal to the curve radius, and drill a hole. Insert a pencil in the hole, and pivot the trammel around the centerpoint, marking the joists for angled cuts.

Variation: For elliptical or irregular curves, temporarily nail vertical anchor boards to the outside joists at the start of the curve. Position a long strip of flexible material, such as hardboard or paneling, inside the anchor boards, then push the strip to create the desired bow. Drive nails into the joists to hold the bow in position, then scribe cutting lines on the tops of the joists.

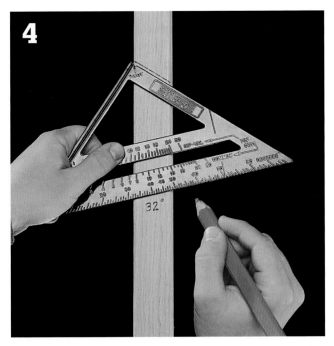

Use a speed square or protractor to determine the bevel angles you will use to cut the joists. Position the square so the top is aligned with the layout mark on the joist, then find the degree measurement by following the edge of the joist down from the pivot point and reading where it intersects the degree scale on the square.

Use a combination square to extend the cutting lines down the front and back faces of the joists. At the outside joists where the curve begins, mark square cutting lines at the point where the circular curve touches the inside edge of the joists.

Cut off each joist with a circular saw set to the proper bevel. Clamp a straightedge to the joist to provide a guide for the foot of the saw. On the outside joists where the curve begins, make 90° cuts.

Where the bevel angle is beyond the range of your circular saw, use a reciprocating saw to cut off the joists.

Decking

The type of decking you choose and the way you install it will impact your deck in several important ways. First, decking serves as a walking surface, so it must be durable, slip resistant and uniformly sized. Wood decking has been the predominant choice for decades, but you may not know that there are many alternative deck materials available, made of recycled or manufactured materials (pages 190 to 191). Aside from lower maintenance requirements, manufactured decking is virtually defect free, and often it can be installed without visible fasteners. Whether you choose wood or composite decking for your project, this chapter will show you how to install it correctly.

Decking can also contribute an aesthetic benefit to your deck, depending on how you lay it. One way to break up the rectilinear shape of a large deck is to install the decking in a parquet or diagonal pattern instead of parallel or perpendicular to the deck frame.

This chapter will teach you about pattern options for decking as well as the various fastening techniques and systems available to you.

In this chapter:

- Decking Patterns
- Laying Decking

Decking Patterns

Decking is an important element of a deck, and it can be installed using a variety of board sizes and design patterns. The decking pattern determines the spacing and layout of the joists. For example, a normal, straight decking pattern requires joists that are spaced 16" on-center. A diagonal decking pattern requires that the joist spacing be 12" on-center. Parquet patterns and some other designs may require extra support, such as double joists or extra blocking. For sturdy, flat decking, use 2 × 4 or 2 × 6 lumber. Thinner lumber is more likely to twist or cup.

Diagonal pattern adds visual interest to a deck. Diagonal patterns require joists that are spaced closer together than straight patterns.

Parquet pattern requires double joists and blocking to provide a supporting surface for attaching the butted ends of decking boards.

Framed opening for a tree requires extra blocking between joists. Short joists are attached to blocking with joist hangers.

Border pattern gives an elegant, finished look to a deck. Install trim joists to support the border decking.

Laying Decking

Buy decking boards that are long enough to span the width of the deck, if possible. If boards must be butted end-to-end, make sure to stagger the joints so they do not overlap from row to row. Predrill the ends of boards to prevent screws or nails from splitting the wood.

Install decking so that there is a ⅛" gap between boards to provide drainage. Boards naturally "cup" as they age. Lay boards with the bark side facing down, so that the cupped surface cannot hold standing water.

General installation instructions for decking materials are shown here. Always follow the installation methods recommended by the manufacturer of the product you select.

Tools & Materials ▸

Tape measure
Circular saw
Screwgun
Hammer
Drill
⅛" twist bit
Pry bar
Chalk line
Jigsaw or handsaw
Decking boards
2½" corrosion-resistant
   deck screws
Galvanized common
   nails (8d, 10d)
Redwood or cedar
   facing boards

How to Lay Decking

Position the first row of decking flush against the house. First decking board should be perfectly straight, and should be precut to proper length. Attach the first decking board by driving a pair of 2½" corrosion-resistant deck screws into each joist.

Position remaining decking boards so that ends overhang outside joists. Space boards about ⅛" apart. Attach boards to each joist with a pair of 2½" deck screws driven into each joist.

Alternate method: Attach decking boards with 10d galvanized common nails. Angle the nails toward each other to improve holding power.

If boards are bowed, use a pry bar to maneuver them into position while fastening.

Drill ⅛" pilot holes in ends of boards before attaching them to outside joists. Pilot holes prevent screws from splitting decking boards at ends.

After every few rows of decking are installed, measure from edge of the decking board to edge of header joist. If measurements show that the last board will not fit flush against the edge of the deck, adjust board spacing.

Adjust board spacing by changing the gaps between boards by a small amount over three or four rows of boards. Very small spacing changes will not be obvious to the eye.

(continued)

7

Use a chalk line to mark the edge of decking flush with the outside of deck. Cut off decking, using a circular saw. Set saw blade ⅛" deeper than thickness of decking so that saw will not cut side of deck. At areas where circular saw cannot reach, finish cutoff with a jigsaw or handsaw.

8

For a more attractive appearance, face the deck with redwood or cedar facing boards. Miter cut corners, and attach boards with deck screws or 8d galvanized nails.

Alternate facing technique: Attach facing boards so that edges of decking overhang facing.

Composite Decking

Lay composite decking as you would wood decking (pages 106 to 107). Position with the factory crown up so water will run off, and space rows ⅛" to ¼" apart for drainage.

Predrill pilot holes at ¾ the diameter of the fasteners, but do not countersink. Composite materials allow fasteners to set themselves. Use spiral shank nails, hot-dipped galvanized ceramic coated screws, or stainless steel nails or deck screws.

Cut away for clarity

Alternate method: Attach composite decking with self-tapping composite screws. These specially designed screws require no pilot holes. If the decking "mushrooms" over the screw head, use a hammer to tap back in place.

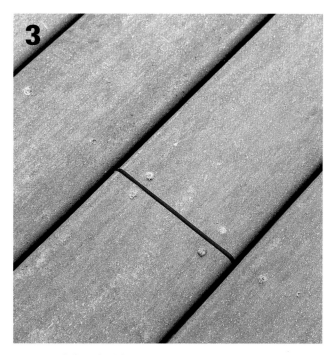

Lay remaining decking. For boards 16-ft. or shorter, leave a gap at deck ends and any butt joints, 1⁄16" for every 20°F difference between the temperature at the time of installation and the expected high temperature for the year.

Tongue-and-groove Decking

Position starter strip at far end of deck. Make sure it is straight and properly aligned. Attach with 2½" galvanized deck screws driven into the lower runner found under the lip of the starter strip.

Fit tongue of a deck board into groove of starter strip. There will be approximately a ¼" gap between the deck board and the starter strip. Fasten the deck board to the joists with 2½" galvanized deck screws, working from the middle out to the sides of the deck.

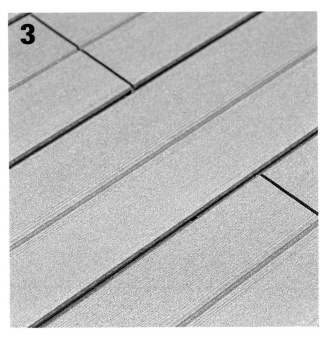

Continue to add decking. To lay deck boards end-to-end, leave a ⅛" gap between them, and make sure any butt joints are centered over a joist.

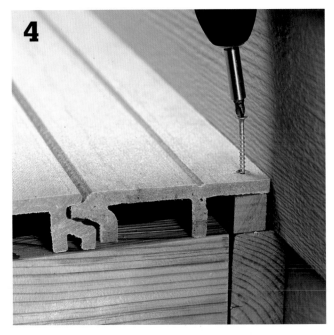

Place final deck board and attach with 2½" galvanized deck screws driven through top of the deck board into the joist. If necessary, rip final board to size, then support the board with a length of 1 × 1 and attach both to the joist. Attach facing boards to conceal exposed ends (photo 4, next page).

T-clip Decking

1

Insert 2" galvanized deck screws into T-clips. Loosely attach one T-clip to the ledger at each joist location.

2

Position a deck board tight against the T-clips. Loosely attach T-clips against bottom lip on front side of deck board, just tight enough to keep the board in place. Fully tighten T-clips at back of board, against the house.

3

Push another deck board tightly against the front T-clips, attach T-clips at front of the new board, then fully tighten the previous set of T-clips. Add another deck board and repeat the process, to the end of the deck.

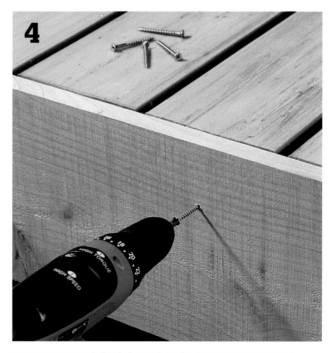

4

Cover exposed deck board ends. Miter cut corners of the facing, and drill pilot holes ¾ the diameter of the screws. Attach with 3" galvanized deck screws.

Fiberglass Deck Systems

Place a length of retaining clips on top of the first joist. Center it on the joist and fasten with 2" galvanized deck screws. Attach lengths of retaining clips to the subsequent joists, so that the clips are perfectly aligned with the first length of clips, creating straight rows.

Place the open face of a decking board perpendicular to the joists, resting on top of a row of clips. Apply firm pressure to the top of the deck board until the decking snaps into place over the retaining clips. Work along the row, snapping the deck board in place. Attach the remaining deck boards in place, snapping each onto a row of retaining clips.

Cut the overhanging ends of the decking boards flush with the outside joists, using a circular saw with a fresh carbide-tipped blade or a masonry cut-off disc.

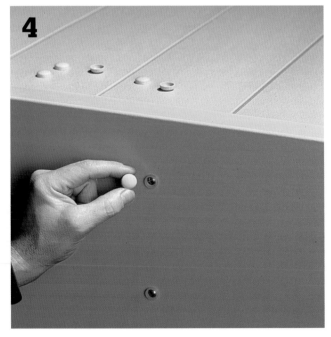

Use 2" galvanized deck screws to attach the pre-fabricated facing, covering the exposed hollow ends and creating a decorative trim. Cover the screw heads with the screw caps.

Decking for a Curve

Install decking for the square portion of the deck, then test-fit decking boards on the curved portion. If necessary, you can make minor adjustments in the spacing to avoid cutting very narrow decking boards at the end of the curve. When satisfied with the layout, scribe cutting lines on the underside of the decking boards, following the edge of the rim joist.

Remove the scribed decking boards, and cut along the cutting lines with a jigsaw. Install the decking boards with deck screws, and smooth the cut edges of the decking boards with a belt sander, if necessary.

Use a Template ▶

Lay the decking boards so the ends overhang the rough opening. Make a cardboard template to draw a cutting line on the deck boards. (When framing for a tree, check with a tree nursery for adequate opening size to provide space for growth.) Cut the decking boards along the marked line, using a jigsaw.

How to Install Decking with Spiked Clips

Drive a spiked clip into the edge of wood decking at joist locations. Use the included fastening block to prevent damage to the spikes.

Drive a deck screw through the hole in the clip and down at an angle through the deck board and into the joist. One screw secures two deck boards at each joist location.

Set the adjacent deck board into place. Tap it against the clips to seat the spikes, using a scrap block and hand maul or sledge hammer.

How to Install Decking with Biscuit-style Clips

Cut a #20 biscuit slot into the edge of deck boards at each joist location using a biscuit joiner (plate joiner). Set the slot height so the bottom edge of the biscuit clip will touch the joist edge.

Insert the biscuit clip into the slot. Drive a deck screw through the hole in the clip and down at an angle through the deck board and into the joist. One screw secures two deck boards at this joist location.

Lay a bead of construction adhesive along the edge of the joist to keep it from squeaking later. Cut slots in the adjacent deck board and fit it over the clips of the previous board.

Tip ▶

The hidden fastener options shown here are excellent alternatives to conventional face-nailing or screwing methods. The biggest advantage is probably aesthetic: you don't have to see row after row of fastener heads any longer with these new installation products. But there are other benefits to hidden fasteners as well. Face-screwed wood decking is more prone to rotting if water collects in the screw head pockets. If you nail the decking down, the nail heads can pop up as wood decking dries and contracts or moves. Hidden fasteners eliminate both of these problems.

If you use spike- or biscuit-style clip systems, be aware that you may need to remove large sections of deck boards in order to replace a damaged or defective board in the future, because the fasteners lock adjacent boards together and hide access to the fasteners.

Stairs

Nearly every deck, including most low-profile styles, requires at least one step, if not more, to reach the deck platform. For complex, multilevel decks or decks built on steep slopes, you may need to build several runs of stairs and possibly a landing. Given the potential risks when using deck stairs, the International Building Code is very specific regarding the size and spacing of treads and risers, the minimum stair width and the structural sizes for stringers. Here's where your local building official can help you steer clear of potential code violations so you can build a safe stair system that will pass inspection.

Since the vertical drop of every deck varies, you'll need to make several calculations to figure out exactly what the layout of your stairs will be. This chapter will show you how. You'll also learn basic stair construction, how to build a longer flight of stairs with a landing, and even how to build a simple box-frame or suspended step when your deck is close to the ground.

In this chapter:

- Building Stairs
- Building Stairways with Landings

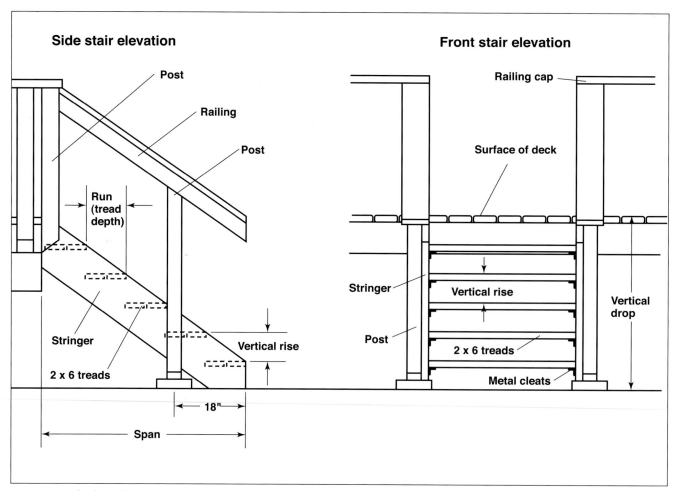

Side stair elevation

Post

Railing

Post

Run (tread depth)

Stringer

2 x 6 treads

Vertical rise

18"

Span

Front stair elevation

Railing cap

Surface of deck

Stringer

Vertical rise

Post

2 x 6 treads

Metal cleats

Vertical drop

A common deck stairway is made from two 2 × 12 stringers and pairs of 2 × 6 treads attached with metal cleats. Posts set 18" back from the end of the stairway help to anchor the stringers and the railings. Calculations needed to build stairs include the number of steps, the rise of each step, the run of each step, and the stairway span.

How to Find Measurements for Stairway Layout ▸

				SAMPLE MEASUREMENTS (39" High Deck)
1.	Find the number of steps: Measure vertical drop from deck surface to ground. Divide by 7. Round off to nearest whole number.	Vertical drop:		39"
		÷ 7 =	÷	5.57"
		Number of steps: =	=	6
2.	Find step rise: Divide the vertical drop by the number of steps.	Vertical drop: =		39"
		Number of steps: ÷	÷	6
		Rise: =	=	6.5"
3.	Find step run: Typical treads made from two 2 × 6s have a run of 11¼". If your design is different, find run by measuring depth of tread, including any space between boards.	Run:		11¼"
4.	Find stairway span: Multiply the run by the number of treads. (Number of treads is always one less than number of steps.)	Run:		11¼"
		Number of treads:	×	5
		Span: =	=	56¼"

Simple Stairs: How to Build a Box-frame Step

Construct a rectangular frame for the step using dimension lumber (2 × 6 lumber is standard). Join the pieces with deck screws. The step must be at least 36" wide and 10" deep. Cut cross blocks and install them inside the frame, spaced every 16".

Dig a flat-bottomed trench, about 4" deep, where the step will rest. Fill the trench with compactible gravel, and pack with a tamper. Set the step in position, then measure and attach deck boards to form the tread of the step.

Simple Stairs: How to Build a Suspended Step

Screw 2 × 4 furring strips against one side of the deck joists where the step joists will be installed. These strips provide an offset so the step joists will not conflict with the joist hangers attached to the beam. Use a reciprocating saw and chisel to make 1½"-wide notches in the rim joist adjacent to the furring strips. *Note: To maintain adequate structural strength, notches in the joists should be no more than 1½" deep.*

Measure and cut step joists, allowing about 3 ft. of nailing surface inside the deck frame, and 10" or more of exposed tread. Make sure the step joists are level with one another, then attach them to the deck joists, using deck screws. Cut and attach deck boards to the tread area of the step.

How to Build Basic Deck Stairs

Use the stairway elevation drawings to find measurements for stair stringers and posts. Use a pencil and framing square to outline where stair stringers will be attached to the side of the deck.

Locate the post footings so they are 18" back from the end of stairway span. Lay a straight 2 × 4 on the deck so that it is level and square to side of deck. Use a plumb bob to mark the ground at centerpoints of footings.

Dig holes and pour footings for posts. Attach metal post anchors to footings and install posts. Check with your building department to find out if 6 × 6 posts are now required.

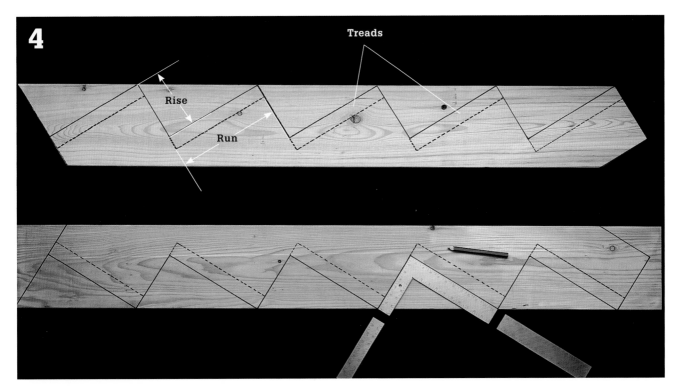

4

Treads

Rise

Run

Lay out stair stringers. Use tape to mark the rise measurement on one leg of a framing square, and the run measurement on the other leg. Beginning at one end of stringer, position the square with tape marks flush to edge of board, and outline the rise and run for each step. Then draw in the tread outline against the bottom of each run line. Use a circular saw to trim ends of stringers as shown.

5

Attach metal tread cleats flush with bottom of each tread outline, using ¼" × 1¼" lag screws. Drill ⅛" pilot holes to prevent the screws from splitting the wood.

6

Attach angle brackets to upper ends of stringers, using 10d joist hanger nails. Brackets should be flush with cut ends of stringers.

(continued)

Position the stair stringers against side of deck, over the stringer outlines. Align top point of stringer flush with the surface of the deck. Attach stringers by nailing the angle brackets to the deck with 10d joist hanger nails.

Drill two ¼" pilot holes through each stringer and into each adjacent post. Counterbore each hole to depth of ½", using a 1" spade bit. Attach stringers to posts with ⅜" × 4" lag screws and washers, using a ratchet wrench or impact driver. Seal screw heads with silicone caulk.

Measure width of stair treads. Cut two 2 × 6s for each tread, using a circular saw.

For each step, position the front 2 × 6 on the tread cleat, so that the front edge is flush with the tread outline on the stringers.

Drill ⅛" pilot holes, then attach the front 2 × 6 to the cleats with ¼" × 1¼" lag screws.

Position the rear 2 × 6 on the cleats, allowing a small space between boards. Use a 16d nail as a spacing guide. Drill ⅛" pilot holes, and attach 2 × 6 to cleats with ¼" × 1¼" lag screws. Repeat for remaining steps.

Stair Variation

Notched stringers precut from pressure-treated wood are available at building centers. Edges of cutout areas should be coated with sealer-preservative to prevent rot.

Construction Details

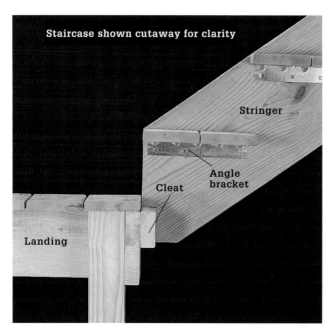

Stringers for the top staircase rest on a 2 × 4 cleat attached to the side of the landing. The stringers are notched to fit around the cleat. On the outside stringers, angle brackets support the treads.

Steps may be boxed in the riser boards, and may have treads that overhang the front edge of the step for a more finished look. Treads should overhang the riser boards by no more than 1".

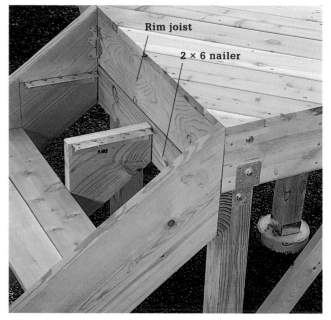

Concrete footings support the stringers for the lower staircase. J-bolts are inserted into the footings while the concrete is still wet. After the footings dry, wooden cleats are attached to the bolts to create surfaces for anchoring the stringers. After the staircase is positioned, the stringers are nailed or screwed to the cleats.

Center stringers are recommended for any staircase that has more than 3 steps or is more than 36" wide. Center stringers are supported by a 2 × 6 nailer attached with metal straps to the bottom of the rim joist. The bottom edge of the nailer is beveled to match the angle of the stringers. The center stringer is attached by driving deck screws through the back of the nailer and into the stringer.

How to Create a Preliminary Layout

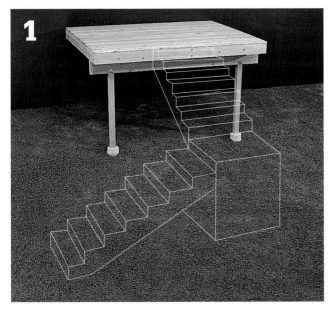

Evaluate your building site and try to visualize which stairway design best fits your needs. When creating a preliminary layout, it is generally best to position the landing so the upper and lower staircases will be of equal length. Select a general design idea.

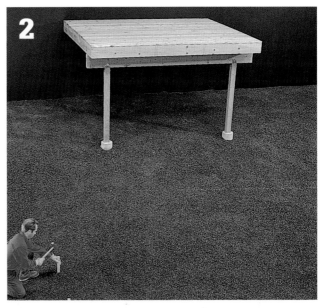

Establish a rough starting point for the stairway on the deck, and an ending point on the ground that conforms with your design. Mark the starting point on the rim joist, and mark the ending point with two stakes, spaced to equal the planned width of your stairway. This is a rough layout only; later calculations will give you the precise measurements.

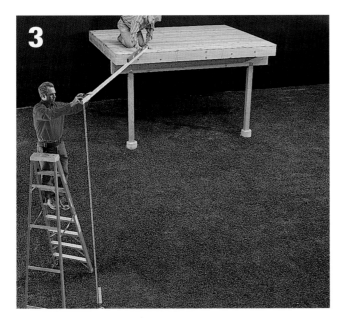

To determine the vertical drop of the stairway, extend a straight 2 × 4 from the starting point on the deck to a spot level with the deck directly over the ending point on the ground. Measure the distance to the ground; this measurement is the total vertical drop. *Note: If the ending point is more than 10 ft. from the starting point, use a mason's string and line level to establish a reference point from which to measure.*

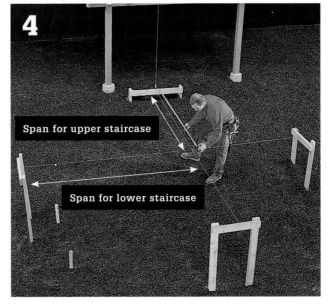

Span for upper staircase

Span for lower staircase

Measure the horizontal span for each staircase. First, use batterboards to establish level layout strings representing the edges of the staircases. Find the span for the upper staircase by measuring from a point directly below the edge of the deck out to the edge of the landing. Measure the span for the lower staircase from the landing to the endpoint.

Create Final Stair Landing Layouts ▸

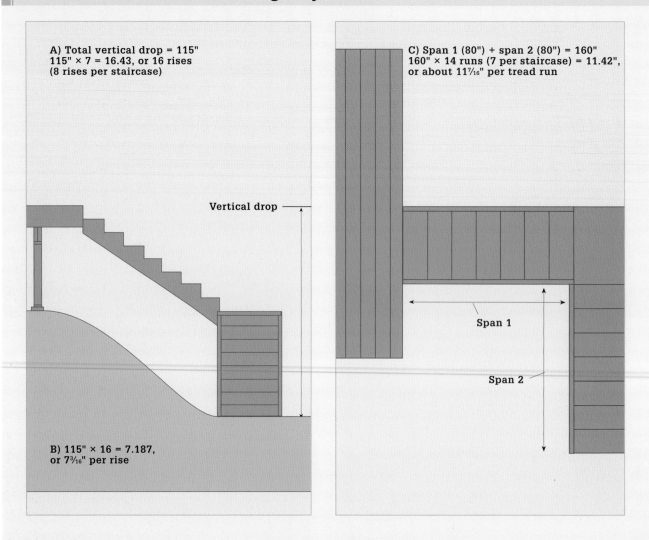

A) Total vertical drop = 115"
115" × 7 = 16.43, or 16 rises
(8 rises per staircase)

Vertical drop

B) 115" × 16 = 7.187,
or 7³⁄₁₆" per rise

C) Span 1 (80") + span 2 (80") = 160"
160" × 14 runs (7 per staircase) = 11.42",
or about 11⁷⁄₁₆" per tread run

Span 1

Span 2

ILLUSTRATIONS ABOVE:

Find the total number of step rises you will need by dividing the vertical drop by 7, rounding off fractions. (A, example above). Next, determine the exact height for each step rise by dividing the vertical drop by the number of rises (B).

Find the horizontal run for each step by adding the spans of both staircases (not including the landing), then dividing by the number of runs (C). Remember that the number of runs in a staircase is always one less than the number of rises.

If the layout does not conform with the guidelines on page 129, adjust the stairway starting point, ending point, or landing, then recalculate the measurements. After finding all dimensions, return to your building site and adjust the layout according to your final plan.

ILLUSTRATIONS NEXT PAGE:

Lay out stringers on 2 × 12 lumber using a carpenter's square. Trim off the waste sections with a circular saw, finishing the notched cuts with a handsaw. In the illustrations on page 133, the waste sections are left unshaded. In standard deck construction, the outside stringers are fitted with metal tread supports that are attached to the inside faces of the stringers. The middle stringer in each flight of stairs is notched to create surfaces that support the stair treads—when cut, these surfaces must align with the tops of the metal tread supports. For the upper staircase stringers, notches are cut at the bottom, front edges to fit over a 2 × 4 cleat that is attached to the landing (see page 125). The top of each notch should lie below the nose of the bottom tread by a distance equal to one rise plus the thickness of a decking board (see next page).

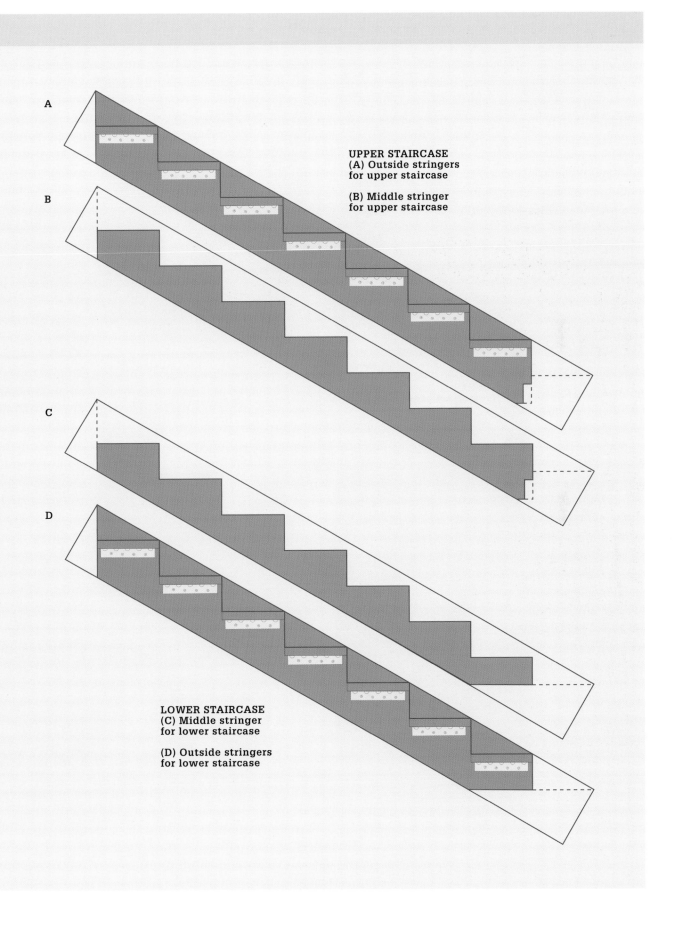

UPPER STAIRCASE
(A) Outside stringers
for upper staircase

(B) Middle stringer
for upper staircase

LOWER STAIRCASE
(C) Middle stringer
for lower staircase

(D) Outside stringers
for lower staircase

How to Build Stairs with a Landing

Begin construction by building the landing. On a flat surface, build the landing frame from 2 × 6 lumber. Join the corners with 3" deck screws, then check for square by measuring diagonals. Adjust the frame until the diagonals are equal, then tack braces across the corners to hold the frame square.

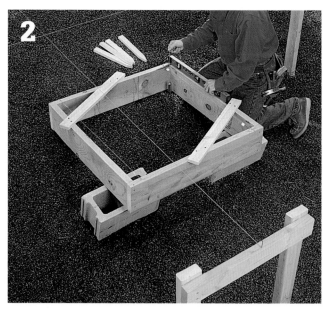

Using your plan drawing, find the exact position of the landing on the ground, then set the frame in position and adjust it for level. Drive stakes to mark locations for the landing posts, using a plumb bob as a guide. Install the footings and posts for the landing.

From the top of the deck, measure down a distance equal to the vertical drop for the upper staircase. Attach a 2 × 4 reference board across the deck posts at this height. Position a straightedge on the reference board and against the landing posts so it is level, and mark the posts at this height. Measure down a distance equal to the thickness of the decking boards, and mark reference lines to indicate where the top of the landing frame will rest.

Attach the landing frame to the posts at the reference lines. Make sure the landing is level, then secure it with joist ties attached to the posts with ⅝" × 3" lag screws. Cut off the posts flush with the top of the landing frame, using a reciprocating saw.

Remove the diagonal braces from the top of the landing frame, then cut and install joists. (For a diagonal decking pattern, space the joists every 12".) Attach the decking boards, and trim them to the edge of the frame.

For extra support and to help prevent sway, create permanent cross braces by attaching 2 × 4 boards diagonally from the bottoms of the posts to the inside of the landing frame. Brace at least two sides of the landing. Remove the temporary braces and stakes holding the posts.

Lay out and cut all stringers for both the upper and lower staircases (page 125). For the center stringers only, cut notches where the treads will rest. Start the notches with a circular saw, then finish the cuts with a handsaw. Measure and cut all tread boards.

Use ¾"-long lag screws to attach angle brackets to the stringers where the treads will rest, then turn the stringers upside down and attach the treads with lag screws. Gaps between tread boards should be no more than ⅜".

(continued)

Dig and pour a concrete footing to support each stringer for the lower staircase. Make sure the footings are level and are the proper height in relation to the landing. Install a metal J-bolt in each footing while the concrete is wet, positioning the bolts so they will be offset about 2" from the stringers. After the concrete dries, cut 2 × 4 footing cleats, drill holes in them, and attach them to the J-bolts using nuts.

Attach a 2 × 6 nailer to the landing to support the center stringer (page 130), then set the staircase in place, making sure the outside stringers are flush with the top of the decking. Use corner brackets and joist-hanger nails to anchor the stringers to the rim joist and nailer. Attach the bottoms of the stringers by nailing them to the footing cleats.

Measure and cut a 2 × 4 cleat to match the width of the upper staircase, including the stringers. Use lag screws to attach the cleat to the rim joist on the landing, flush with the tops of the joists. Notch the bottoms of all stringers to fit around the cleat (page 130), and attach angle brackets on the stringers to support the treads.

To support the center stringer at the top of the staircase, measure and cut a 2 × 6 nailer equal to the width of the staircase. Attach the nailer to the rim joist with metal straps and screws.

Position the stringers so they rest on the landing cleat. Make sure the stringers are level and properly spaced, then toenail the bottoms of the stringers into the cleat, using galvanized 16d nails. At the top of the staircase, use angle brackets to attach the outside stringers to the rim joist and the middle stringer to the nailer.

Measure, cut, and position tread boards over the angle brackets, then attach them from below, using ¾"-long lag screws. The gap between tread boards should be no more than ⅜". After completing the stairway, install railings (pages 144 to 147).

Deck Railings

Decks that are built 30 inches above the ground or higher must have a system of railings installed around their perimeter. Building codes dictate the important spacing and height requirements for railings, but what you may not know is that wood isn't the only option from which to build them. Granted, traditional wooden railings are quick to build and relatively affordable, but there are other exciting and attractive alternatives. This chapter will show you a variety of different railing systems, including those made with prefabricated composite parts, steel cable, clear glass panels and copper tubing. With a measure of creativity on your part, railings can be a showcase design feature of your new deck and not just a means of preventing injuries.

This chapter will also teach you how to outfit your deck stairs with handrails and balusters and even shape a curved railing using several challenging woodworking techniques.

In this chapter:

- Deck Railing Basics
- Curved Railings
- Composite Railing Systems
- Glass-panel Railings
- Steel Cable Railings
- Copper Tube Railings

Deck Railing Basics

Railings must be sturdy and firmly attached to the framing members of the deck. Never attach railing posts to the surface decking. Check local building codes for guidelines regarding railing construction. Most codes require that railings be at least 36" above decking. Vertical balusters should be spaced no more than 4" apart. In some areas, a grippable handrail may be required for any stairway over four treads. Check with your local building inspector for the building codes in your area.

Tools & Materials ▸

Tape measure
Pencil
Power miter saw
Drill
Twist bits (⅛", ¼")
1" spade bit
Combination square
Awl
Ratchet wrench
Caulk gun
Reciprocating saw
 or circular saw
Jigsaw with wood-
 cutting blade

Level
Railing lumber
 (4 × 4s, 2 × 6s,
 2 × 4s, 2 × 2s)
Clear sealer-
 preservative
⅜ × 4" lag screws
 and 1" washers
Silicone caulk
2½" corrosion-
 resistant
 deck screws
10d galvanized
 common nails

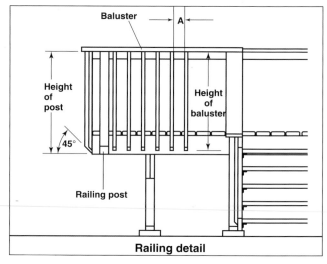

Refer to your deck design plan for spacing (A) and length of railing posts and balusters. Posts should be spaced no more than 6 feet apart.

Railings are mandatory safety features for any deck that's more than 30 inches above grade. There are numerous code issues and stipulations that will dictate how you build your deck railings. Consult with your local building inspector for any code clarification you may need.

Types of Railings

 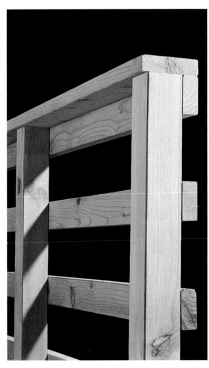 

Vertical balusters with posts and rails are a good choice for houses with strong vertical lines. A vertical baluster railing like the one shown above is a good choice where children will be present.

Horizontal railings are often used on low, ranch-style homes. Horizontal railings are made of vertical posts, two or more wide horizontal rails, and a railing cap.

Lattice panels add a decorative touch to a deck. They also provide extra privacy.

Railing Codes ▸

Railings usually are required by building code on any deck that is more than 30" high. Select a railing design that fits the style of your home.

For example, on a low, ranch-style house, choose a deck railing with wide, horizontal rails. On a Tudor-style home with a steep roof, choose a railing with closely spaced, vertical balusters. See pages 156 to 169 for information on how to build other railing styles, including a curved railing.

Some codes may require easily gripped hand rails for stairways (page 155). Check with your local building inspector.

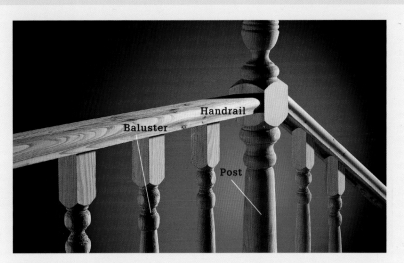

Preshaped products let you easily build decorative deck railings. Railing products include shaped handrails, balusters, and posts.

How to Install a Wood Deck Railing

1

Measure and cut 4 × 4 posts, using a power miter saw or circular saw. Cut off tops of the posts square, and cut the bottoms at 45° angle. Seal cut ends of lumber with clear sealer-preservative.

2

Measure and cut balusters for main deck, using a power miter saw or circular saw. Cut off tops of the balusters square, and cut bottoms at 45° angle. Seal cut ends of lumber with clear sealer-preservative.

3

Drill two ¼" pilot holes spaced 2" apart through bottom end of each post. Counterbore each pilot hole to ½" depth, using a 1" spade bit.

4

Drill two ⅛" pilot holes spaced 4" apart near bottom end of each baluster. Drill two ⅛" pilot holes at top of each baluster, spaced 1½" apart.

5

Measure and mark position of posts around the outside of the deck, using a combination square as a guide. Plan to install a post on outside edge of each stair stringer.

6

Position each post with beveled end flush with bottom of deck. Plumb post with a level. Insert a screwdriver or nail into pilot holes and mark side of deck.

7

Remove post and drill ¼" pilot holes into side of deck.

8

Attach railing posts to side of deck with ⅜" × 4" lag screws and washers, using a ratchet wrench or impact driver. Seal screw heads with silicone caulk.

9

Measure and cut 2 × 4 side rails. Position rails with edges flush to tops of posts, and attach to posts with 2½" corrosion-resistant deck screws.

(continued)

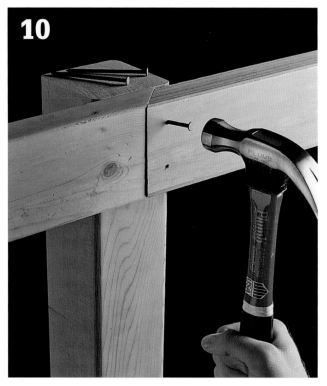

Join 2 × 4s for long rails by cutting ends at 45º angles. Drill ¹⁄₁₆" pilot holes to prevent nails from splitting end grain, and attach rails with 10d galvanized nails. (Screws may split mitered ends.)

Attach ends of rails to stairway posts, flush with edges of posts, as shown. Drill ⅛" pilot holes, and attach rails with 2½" deck screws.

At stairway, measure from surface of decking to the top of the upper stairway post (A).

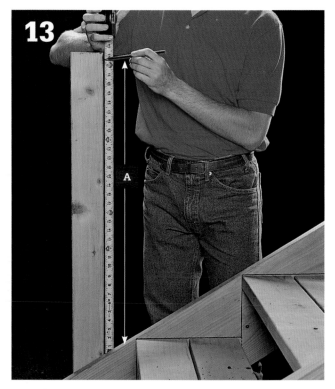

Transfer measurement A to lower stairway post, measuring from the edge of the stair stringer.

14

Rail parallel

Position 2 × 4 rail against inside of stairway posts. Align rail with top rear corner of top post and with the pencil mark on the lower post. Have a helper attach rail temporarily with 2½" deck screws.

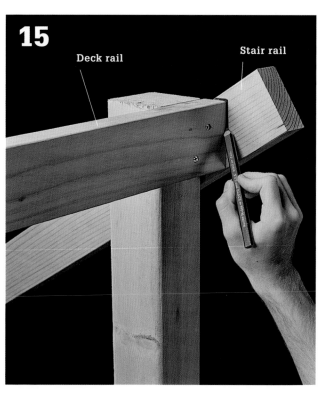

15

Deck rail

Stair rail

Mark the outline of the post and the deck rail on the back side of the stairway rail.

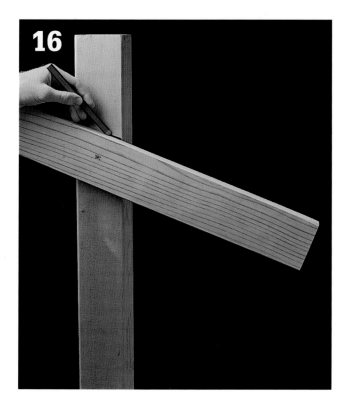

16

Mark the outline of the stairway rail on the lower stairway post.

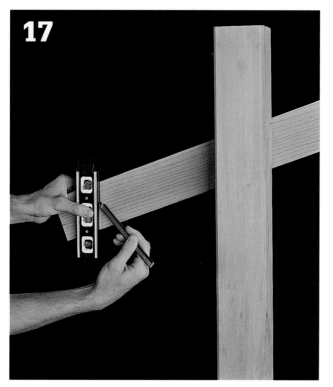

17

Use a level to mark a plumb cutoff line at the bottom end of the stairway rail. Remove the rail.

(continued)

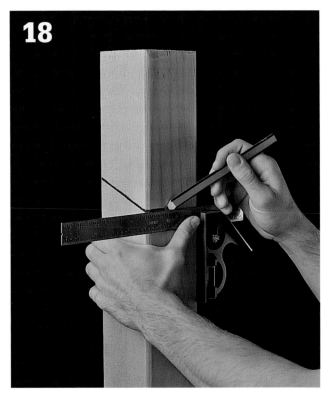

Extend the pencil lines across both sides of the stairway post, using a combination square as a guide.

Cut off lower stairway post along diagonal cutoff line, using a reciprocating saw or circular saw.

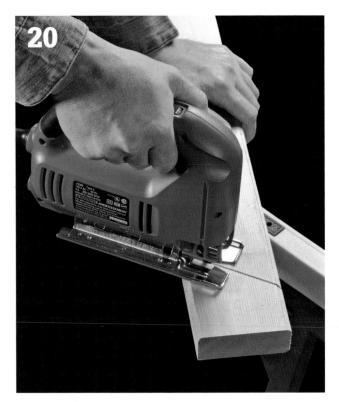

Use a jigsaw to cut the stairway rail along the marked outlines.

Position the stairway rail flush against top edge of posts. Drill ⅛" pilot holes, then attach rail to posts with 2½" deck screws.

22

Use a spacer block to ensure equal spacing between balusters. Beginning next to a plumb railing post, position each baluster tight against spacer block, with top of baluster flush to top of rail. Attach each baluster with 2½" deck screws.

23

For stairway, position baluster against stringer and rail, and adjust for plumb. Draw diagonal cutoff line on top of baluster, using top of stair rail as a guide. Cut baluster on marked line, using power miter saw. Seal ends with clear sealer-preservative.

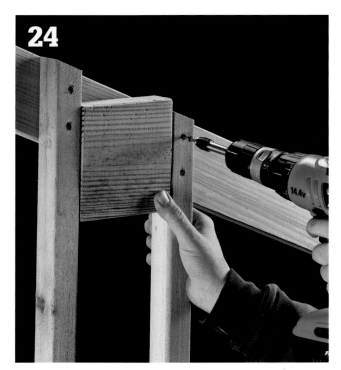

24

Beginning next to upper stairway post, position each baluster tight against spacer block, with top flush to top of stair rail. Attach baluster with 2½" deck screws.

25

Position 2 × 6 cap so edge is flush with inside edge of rail. Drill ⅛" pilot holes, and attach cap to rail with 2½" deck screws driven every 12". Also drive screws into each post and into every third baluster. For long caps, bevel ends at 45°. Drill 1/16" pilot holes, and attach at post using 10d nails.

(continued)

26

At corners, miter ends of railing cap at 45°. Drill ⅛" pilot holes, and attach cap to post with 2½" deck screws.

27

At top of stairs, cut cap so that it is flush with stairway rail. Drill ⅛" pilot holes and attach cap with 2½" deck screws.

28

Measure and cut cap for stairway rail. Mark outline of post on side of cap, and bevel cut the ends of the cap.

29

Position cap over the stairway rail and balusters so that edge of cap is flush with inside edge of rail. Drill ⅛" pilot holes, and attach cap to rail with 2½" deck screws driven every 12". Also drive screws through cap into stair post and into every third baluster.

Wood Railing Style Variations

Vertical baluster railing is a popular style because it complements most house styles. To improve the strength and appearance of the railing, the advanced variation shown here uses a "false mortise" design. The 2 × 2 balusters are mounted on 2 × 2 horizontal rails that slide into mortises notched into the posts (see page 150).

Horizontal railing visually complements modern ranch-style houses with predominantly horizontal lines. For improved strength and a more attractive appearance, the style shown here features 1 × 4 rails set on edge into dadoes cut in the faces of the posts. A cap rail running over all posts and top rails helps unify and strengthen the railing (see page 151).

Wall-style railing is framed with short 2 × 4 stud walls attached flush with the edges of the deck. The stud walls and rim joists are then covered with siding materials, usually chosen to match the siding on the house. A wall-style railing creates a more private space and visually draws the deck into the home, providing a unified appearance (see pages 152 to 153).

Stairway railings are required for any stairway with more than three steps. They are usually designed to match the style used on the deck railing (see pages 154 to 155).

How to Build a Vertical Baluster Railing

Cut 4 × 4 railing posts to size (at least 36", plus the height of the deck rim joists). Lay out and mark partial dadoes 1½" wide and 2½" long where the horizontal 2 × 2 rails will fit. Use a circular saw set to ½" blade depth to make a series of cuts from the edge of the post to the end of layout marks, then use a chisel to clean out the dadoes and square them off. On corner posts, cut dadoes on adjoining sides of the post.

Attach the posts inside the rim joists. To find the length for the rails, measure between the bases of the posts, then add 1" for the ½" dadoes on each post. Measure and cut all balusters. Install the surface boards before continuing with railing construction.

Assemble the rails and balusters on a flat surface. Position the balusters at regular intervals (no more than 4" apart), and secure them by driving 2½" deck screws through the rails. A spacing block cut to match the desired gap can make this easier.

Slide the assembled railings into the post dadoes, and toenail them in position with galvanized casing nails. Cut plugs to fit the exposed dadoes, and glue them in place. The resulting joint should resemble a mortise-and-tenon.

Measure and cut the 2 × 6 cap rails, then secure them by driving 2" deck screws up through the top rail. At corners, miter-cut the cap rails to form miter joints.

How to Build a Notched Deck Railing

Cut all 4 × 4 posts to length, then clamp them together to lay out 3½"-wide × ¾"-deep dadoes for the horizontal rails. For corner posts, cut dadoes on adjacent faces of the post. Cut the dadoes by making a series of parallel cuts, about ¼" apart, between the layout marks.

Knock out the waste wood between the layout marks, using a hammer, then use a chisel to smooth the bottom of each dado. Attach the posts inside the rim joists. Install decking before continuing with railing construction.

Determine the length of 1 × 4 rails by measuring between the bases of the posts. Cut rails to length, then nail them in place using 8d splitless cedar siding nails. At corners, bevel-cut the ends of the rails to form miter joints. If the rails butt together, the joint should fall at the center of a post.

Cleat

Measure and cut 2 × 2 cleats and attach them between the posts, flush with the top rail, using galvanized casing nails. Then, measure and cut cap rails, and position and attach them by driving 2" deck screws up through the cleats. At corners, miter-cut the ends of the cap rails.

How to Build a Sided Railing

Cut the posts to length, using a circular saw or portable miter saw. If your saw does not have enough cutting capacity, make the cut in two passes.

Attach the posts inside the rim joists with lag screws or lag bolts, then add blocking between joists to reinforce the posts. Install decking before continuing with railing construction.

Blocking goes here

Build a 2 x 4 stud wall to match the planned height of your railing. Space studs 16" on center, and attach them by driving deck screws through the top plate and sole plate.

Position the stud wall on the deck, flush with the edges of the rim joists, then anchor it by driving 3" deck screws down through the sole plate. At corners, screw the studs of adjoining walls together. At open ends, screw the end studs to posts.

5

At corners, attach 2 × 4 nailers flush with the inside and outside edges of the top plate and sole plate to provide a nailing surface for attaching trim boards and siding materials.

6

On inside corners, attach a 2 × 2 trim strip, using 10d splitless cedar siding nails. Siding materials will be butted against this trim strip.

7

On outside corners, attach 1 × 4 trim boards on both sides, so one board overlaps the end grain of the other. The trim boards should extend down over the rim joist. Also attach trim boards around posts.

8

Cut and position cap rails on the top rail, then secure them with 2" deck screws driven up through the rail. Railing caps should be mitered at the corners.

9

Attach siding materials to the inside and outside faces of the wall, using splitless cedar siding nails. Snap level chalk lines for reference, and try to match the reveal used on your house siding; the first course should overhang the rim joist slightly. Where joints are necessary, stagger them from course to course so they do not fall on the same studs.

How to Build an Angled Stair Railing

Use a combination square to mark the face of the top stairway post, where the railings will fit. For most horizontal stairway designs, the top stairway rail should start level with the second deck rail. Mark the other stairway posts at the same level.

Position a rail board against the faces of the posts, with the bottom edge against the stringer, then scribe angled cutting lines across the rail along the inside edges of the posts. Cut the rail at these lines, then cut the remaining rails to match.

Secure the rails to the posts, with galvanized metal L-brackets attached to the insides of the rails.

Measure and cut a 2 × 2 cleat, and attach it flush with the top inside edge of the top rail, using 2" deck screws. Anchor the cleat to the posts by toenailing with galvanized casing nails.

Measure and cut the cap rail to fit over the top rail and cleat. At the bottom of the railing, cut the post at an angle and attach the cap rail so it overhangs the post slightly. Secure the cap rail by driving 2" deck screws up through the cleat.

Measure and cut a grippable handrail, attaching it to the posts with mounting brackets. Miter cut the ends, and create a return back to the post by cutting another mitered section of handrail and nailing it in place between the handrail and post (right).

Grippable Handrails ▸

Grippable handrails are required for stairways with more than two treads. The handrail should be shaped so the grippable portion is between 1¼" and 2" in diameter, and should be angled into posts at the ends. The top of the handrail should be 34" to 38" above the stair treads, measured from the nose of a step.

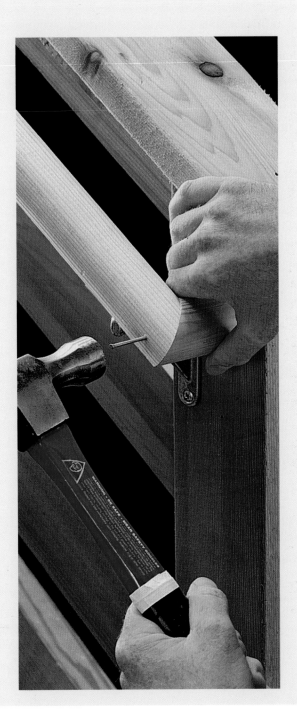

Curved Railings

Laying out and constructing a curved railing requires a basic understanding of geometry and the ability to make detailed drawings using a compass, protractor, and a special measuring tool called a scale ruler.

Creating a curved railing is a fairly advanced technique, but the results are worth the effort. Making the top rail involves bending and gluing thinner strips of wood together around the deck's curved rim joist, which acts like a bending form. You'll need lots of medium-sized clamps on hand to hold the railing in the proper shape while it dries. The cap rail is formed by joining several mitered pieces of lumber together, end to end, to form an oversized blank, then cutting out the curved shape.

The method for constructing a curved cap rail shown on the following pages works only for symmetrical, curves—quarter circles, half circles, or full circles. If your deck has irregular or elliptical curves, creating a cap rail is very difficult. For these curves, it is best to limit the railing design to include only balusters and a laminated top rail.

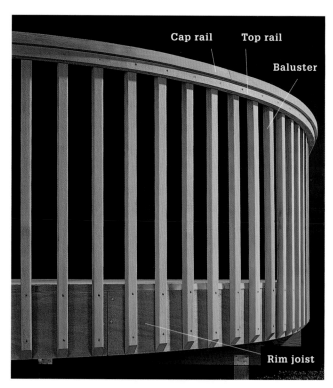

Components of a curved railing include: vertical balusters attached to the curved rim joist, a top rail built from laminated layers of plywood, and a curved cap rail. The cap rail is constructed by laying out mitered sections of 2 × 12 lumber, marking a curved shape, and cutting it out with a jigsaw.

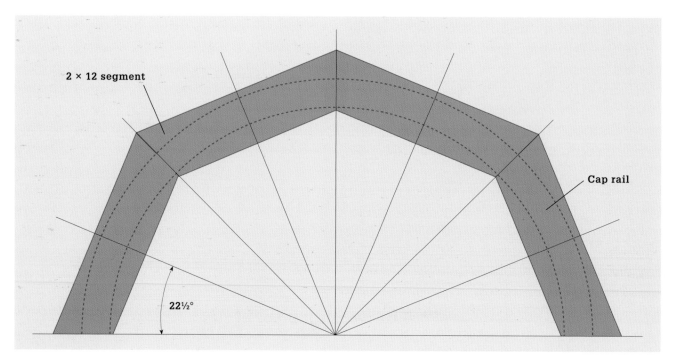

Curved cap rail is created from mitered segments of 2 × 12 lumber. After positioning the 2 × 12 segments end to end, the shape of the 6"-wide cap rail is outlined on the pieces. For a semicircle with a radius of up to 7 ft., four 2 × 12 segments will be needed, with ends mitered at 22½°. For a semicircle with a larger radius, you will need eight segments, with ends mitered at 11¼°.

How to Build a Curved Railing

To create a curved top rail, use exterior glue to laminate four 1½"-wide strips of ⅜"-thick cedar plywood together, using the curved rim joist of the deck as a bending form. First, cover the rim joist with kraft paper for protection. Then, begin wrapping strips of plywood around the rim joist. Clamp each strip in position, starting at one end of the curve. The strips should differ in length to ensure that butt joints will be staggered from layer to layer.

Continue working your way around the rim joist, toward the other end. Make sure to apply clamps on both sides of the butt joints where plywood strips meet. Cut the last strips slightly long, then trim the laminated rail to the correct length after the glue has set. For extra strength, drive 1" deck screws through the rail at 12" intervals after all strips are glued together. Unclamp the rail, and sand the top and bottom edges smooth.

Install posts at the square corners of the deck. Then, cut 2 × 2 balusters to length, beveling the bottom ends at 45°. Attach the balusters to the rim joist with 2½" deck screws, using a spacer to maintain even intervals. Clamp the curved top rail to the tops of the balusters and posts, then attach it with deck screws.

After the top rail and balusters are in place, attach 2 × 2 top rails to the balusters in the straight sections of the deck. The ends of the straight top rails should be flush against the ends of the curved top rail. Now, measure the distance between the inside faces of the balusters at each end of the curve. Divide this distance in half to find the required radius for the curved cap rail.

(continued)

Using a scale of 1" equals 1 ft., make a diagram of the deck. (A scale ruler makes this job easier.) First, draw the arc of the deck with a compass, using the radius measurement found in step 4. Divide the curved portion of the deck into an even number of equal sections by using a protractor to draw radius lines from the center of the curve. For a semicircular curve, it is usually sufficient to draw eight radius lines, angled at 22½° to one another. (For a deck with a radius of more than 7 ft., you may need to divide the semicircle into 16 portions, with radius lines angled at 11¼°.)

From the point where one of the radius lines intersects the curved outline of the deck, use the scale ruler to mark points 5½" above and 5½" below the intersection. From these points, use a protractor to draw perpendicular lines to the adjoining radius lines. The polygon outlined by the perpendicular lines and the adjoining radius lines represents the shape and size for all of the 2 × 12 segments that will be used to construct the cap rail.

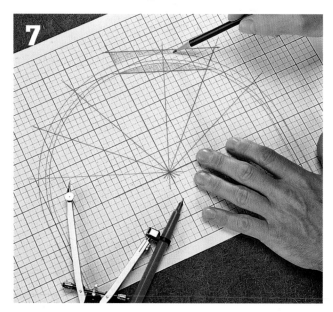

Draw a pair of parallel arcs 5½" apart, representing the curved cap railing, inside the outline for the 2 × 12 segments. Shade the portion of the drawing that lies between the straight parallel lines and the two adjacent radius lines. This area represents the shape and size for each of the angled 2 × 12 segments. Measure the angle of the miter at the ends of the board; in this example, the segments are mitered at 22½°.

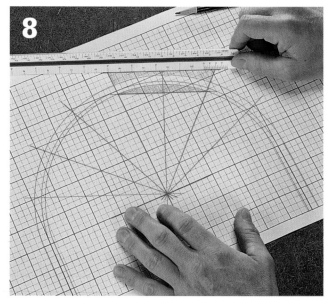

Measure the length of the long edge; this number is the overall length for each of the 2 × 12 segments you will be cutting. Using this highlighted area, determine how many segments you will need to complete the curve. For a semicircular curve with a radius of up to 7 ft., four segments are required, with ends mitered at 22½°. For curves with a larger radius, you need eight segments, with ends mitered at 11¼°.

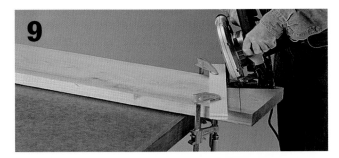

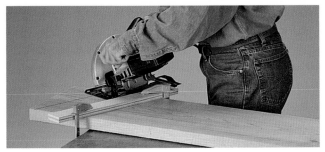

Measure and mark 2 × 12 lumber for the cap rail segments, with ends angled inward at 22½° from perpendicular. Set the blade on your circular saw or tablesaw to a 15° bevel, then make compound miter cuts along the marked lines. When cut to compound miters, the segments will form overlapping scarf joints that are less likely to reveal gaps between the boards.

Arrange the cap rail segments over the curved deck railing, and adjust the pieces, if necessary, so they are centered over the top rail. When you are satisfied with the layout, temporarily attach the segments in place by driving 2" deck screws up through the curved top rail. Measure and install the 2 × 6 cap railing for the straight portion of the railing.

Temporarily nail or clamp a long sturdy board between the sides at the start of the curve. Build a long compass, called a *trammel*, by nailing one end of a long 1 × 2 to a 1 ft.-long piece of 1 × 4. Measure from the nail out along the arm of the trammel, and drill holes at the desired radius measurements; for our application, there will be two holes, 5½" apart, representing the width of the finished cap rail. Attach the 1 × 4 base of the trammel to the temporary board so the nail point is at the centerpoint of the deck rail curve, then insert a pencil through one of the holes in the trammel arm. Pivot the arm of the trammel around the cap rail, scribing a cutting line. Move the pencil to the other hole, and scribe a second line.

Remove the trammel, and unscrew the cap rail segments. Use a jigsaw to cut along the scribed lines, then reposition the curved cap rail pieces over the top rail. Secure the cap rail by applying exterior adhesive to the joints and driving 2½" deck screws up through the top rail. Use a belt sander to remove saw marks.

Decorative Railing Options ▸

Even if you are committed to using wood posts and railings for your deck, there are numerous ways to customize your railing system to make it look fresh and different from other decks. One dramatic step you can take is to choose an unusual material option for the balusters. Balusters are available in various metals, including aluminum, stainless or powder-coated steel, copper and iron. Metal balusters are fabricated in straight or contoured styles as well as turned and architectural profiles. They install into holes in wooden top and bottom rails or attach with screws. Strips of tempered glass are another baluster option, and they fasten in place with screws or slip into grooves in the rails. Or, fill the spaces between posts and rails with brightly colored outdoor fabric. It can be ordered with metal grommets installed so you tie it in place with weather-resistant rope.

If you use metal balusters, consider adding a centerpiece railing between them. These unique railings are made in various fleur de lis, classic and nouveau patterns. They'll add shape and distinctiveness to your baluster pattern.

Wooden posts need not be drab, either. One option is to cover them with composite or vinyl sleeves in various colors or outfit them with a sleeve that looks like stacked stone. Instead of running hand rails over the top of your deck posts, let them extend above the railings and install post caps or decorative wood finials. Caps and finials simply fit over the tops of posts and nail or screw in place. Caps are widely available from home centers in copper or stainless steel. You can also order them made from stained glass or as low-voltage solar lights. Then, add a little flair to the bottoms of your posts with one-piece, composite trim skirts in decorative profiles.

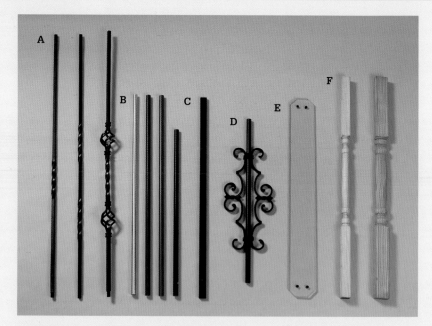

Balusters are available in a variety of styles and material options. Metal balusters are fabricated into many contoured profiles (A). You can also buy tubular styles (B) made of aluminum, stainless steel, and copper, or with a painted finish. Flat-bar balusters (C) or decorative centerpiece railings (D) are other options, as well as strips of tempered glass (E). Wood balusters (F) are more economical than other styles, but they still lend a nicely crafted touch.

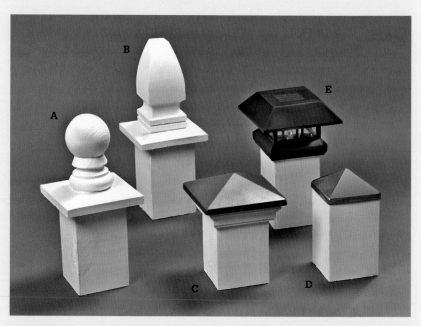

Dress up your deck railing posts with decorative top caps. You'll find them in various ball (A) and finial (B) shapes. Consider topping off your posts with paint (C) or copper (D), or maybe low-voltage or solar powered cap lights (E). Top caps will also help your wooden posts last longer by preventing water from wicking down into the end grain, leading to rot.

Post caps are available in a variety of styles and made of metal, composites or wood. Aside from adding a decorative touch, they also extend the life of the posts by preventing water from wicking down into the end grain.

If you'd prefer not to build your railing from scratch, you can buy PVC or other composite railing systems that are simple to install and long lasting. Another advantage is you'll never need to stain or paint them.

Tempered glass railings are an excellent choice if your deck offers an impressive view. There are no balusters or handrails to peek through or over—just clear "windows" to the world beyond.

Contoured metal balusters will give your deck a fresh, contemporary twist. They attach with screws, just like wooden balusters.

Spindle-style, turned balusters are available in various metal tones and colors. They can lend a tailored effect to wooden railings.

Ordinary wooden deck railings can make you feel like you're "behind bars," but they're not the only option anymore. Today's tempered glass railing systems offer the same safety as wood balusters but with the added advantage of a virtually unobstructed view.

Composite Railing Systems

Several manufacturers of composite decking now offer composite railing kits that are easy to install by do-it-yourselfers. Aside from the advantages of using reclaimed and recycled materials for your railings, composites are also virtually maintenance free and come in a variety of styles and colors. Some railing systems are packaged in kits with all the components necessary to build six-ft. sections of railing. Other companies sell the pieces individually, and you may need to cut the components to size to fit your railing application (see resources, p. 315).

Tools & Materials ▸

Tape measure	Bracket tool
Level	Lag screws
Ratchet and sockets or	Posts
impact driver	Balusters
Miter saw	Rail cap
Drill/driver	Stringers
16-gauge pneumatic nailer	

Composite deck railing systems are very durable and require only minimal maintenance.

How to Install a Composite Railing

Fasten composite railing posts to the deck rim joists with pairs of ½-in.-diameter, countersunk bolts, washers and nuts. Position the posts 72 inches on center. Do not notch the posts.

Install railing support brackets, if applicable, to the posts using corrosion-resistant deck screws. For the railing system shown here, an assembly bracket tool sets the placement of the brackets on the posts without measuring.

Assemble the balusters, top and bottom rails into the correct configuration on a flat work surface. Again, the assembly tool shown here sets the spacing of the balusters. Fasten the bottom rails to the balusters with 16-gauge pneumatic nails or deck screws, according the manufacturer's recommendations.

Fasten the top rails to the balusters with 16-gauge pneumatic nails.

Place the assembled railing section onto the railing support brackets and check it for level. Drive pairs of deck screws up though the support bracket holes and into the handrail. Toenail the bottom rail to the post with 16-gauge pneumatic nails.

Glass-panel Railings

For the ultimate in unobstructed viewing, you can install a glass-panel railing system on your deck and avoid balusters altogether. The system shown here (see Resources, page 315) is quite manageable to install without special tools. It consists of a framework of aluminum posts, and top and bottom rails that fasten together with screws. Extruded vinyl liner inserts that fit inside the top and bottom rails hold the glass without fasteners. Tempered glass panels that are at least ¼-in. thick will meet building codes, provided the railing posts are spaced 5 ft. on center. It is recommended that you assemble the railing framework first, then measure and order the glass panels to fit the rail openings.

Tools & Materials ▶

Tape measure
Level
Ratchet and sockets or impact driver
Drill/driver
Posts
Post brackets
Tempered glass panels
Fasteners
Railings
Stringers

Tempered glass panels are both do-it-yourself friendly and code approved, provided you install them according to manufacturer guidelines.

How to Install a Glass-panel Railing

Once you've determined the layout of the deck posts, fasten the post brackets to the deck with lag screws. Install all the posts and bottom rails before proceeding.

Insert the top post sleeves into the post ends, then measure and cut the top rails to length. Assemble the rails and sleeves, fastening the parts with screws. Check each post for plumb with a level before driving the attachment screws, and adjust if necessary.

Measure the length of the top rail inner channels, and cut glass insert strips to fit. Fasten the glass rail brackets to the posts with screws.

Measure the distance between the glass inserts and add ¾". to this length to determine the height of the glass panels. Measure the distance between posts and subtract 3 to 6". from this measurement to find the glass panel width, less air gaps. Order your glass. Install the bottom rails on the brackets.

Slip each glass panel into the top insert, swing it into place over the bottom insert and lower it into the bottom channel to rest on the rubber setting blocks. No further attachment is required.

Steel Cable Railings

A series of braided steel cables can replace ordinary wood balusters and give your deck a clean, contemporary look. Posts must be spaced closely together to handle the cable tension and ensure safety.

Another railing option that can improve the view from your deck is to use braided steel cables between the railing posts. Here, lengths of cable pass continuously through holes in the posts and tension is created with a special threaded fitting on the cable end. Cables must be spaced no more than 3 in. apart, with railing posts located 3 ft. on center. You can buy prefabricated metal posts as we show here, or make them from wood. The endmost posts should be made of 4 × 6 lumber to handle the cable tension, although the intermediate posts can be conventionally sized. You'll also need to install a 2 × 6 cap rail securely to all posts and add 1 × 4 blocking under the cap rail to provide additional lateral reinforcement.

Tools & Materials ▸

Measuring tape
Level
Drill/driver
Hack saw
Cable cutters

Self-locking pliers
Wrenches
Electric grinder
Cable-lacing needle

Tip ▸

Cut off the excess threaded bolt at the nut with a hack saw. Grind or file away any sharp edges.

How to Install Cable Railings

If you install flanged metal posts, secure them to the deck's framing with stainless steel lag screws and washers.

Drill holes through the railing posts to fit the cables, threaded end fittings, and quick connect locking fittings. Pass the terminal threaded ends of the cables through one railing end post and install washer nuts about ¼" onto the threads.

Feed the cables through the intermediate posts and the opposite end post. Work systematically to prevent tangling the cables. A cable-lacing needle will make it easier to pass cables through each post without snagging it. Attach cap rails (inset).

Slip a self-locking fitting over the end of each cable and seat the fitting in the cable hole in the post. You may need to counterbore this hole first to accommodate the fitting. Pull the cable tight. Jaws inside the fitting will prevent the cable from becoming slack again.

Tighten each cable nut with a wrench, starting from the center cable and working outward. A locking pliers will keep the cable from twisting as you tighten the nut. Tighten the nut until you cannot flex the cables more than 4" apart.

Cut off the excess cable at the quick-connect fitting end with a cable cutter or hack saw. Grind the end of the cable flush with the fitting, and cover it with a snap-on end cap.

Copper Tube Railings

Use ¾" copper tubing available in the plumbing section of building centers for decorative balusters in a railing. Over time, the copper will oxidize and develop an attractive green patina. Metal balusters coated in colors also are available from some manufacturers. If you can't find them at your local building center, manufacturers and suppliers can be found on the Internet. In some areas, notching 4 × 4 posts to attach them to your deck (as shown here) may not be allowed by local codes. Inquire at your local building department for the restrictions in your area.

How to Build Copper Tube Railings

Lay out and attach railing posts as you would for traditional railings. Measure and cut pairs of 2 × 4 rails to fit between post faces or in notches cut in the post faces.

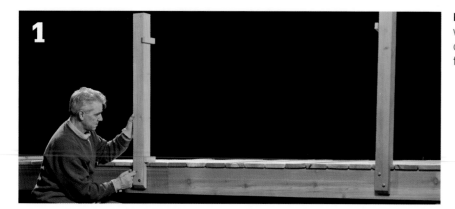

On one edge of an 8-ft. 2 × 4, lay out and mark hole locations every 4½", beginning at the centerpoint and working towards the ends. Use this board as a story pole to create consistent spacing between balusters. Clamp the story pole to each rail pair, aligning the centerpoint of the rails with that of the story pole. If the hole locations fall within 1½" of the ends, adjust the rails, as necessary. Transfer marks to the rails using a speed square.

Drill a ¾"-diameter hole ¾" deep at each location using a portable drill guide and Forstner bit.

Apply a small amount of silicone caulk in each hole in the bottom rail and insert a baluster. The caulk prevents moisture penetration.

Lay a 1 × 4 under the baluster ends to hold them up uniformly. Brace the bottom end so it won't move, then fit the top rail over the baluster ends. A helper will make this much easier. Set the assembly upright, and hammer against a scrap block placed on the top rail to fully seat the balusters in both rails.

For stair rails, mark hole locations that are 5½" apart on center. Turn the top rail 180° and flip it upside down before clamping the rails together. Begin marking at the centerpoint of the rails. Drill holes for the balusters with the clamped rail pair resting on the stair treads. Use a level to set the proper angle for the drill guide if necessary.

Install each rail assembly between the appropriate posts, using 2½" deck screws. Attach cap rails following the methods shown on pages 147 to 148.

Finishing & Maintaining Your Deck

As outdoor structures, decks are constantly subjected to the elements, insect damage, and the wear and tear of foot traffic. In order to prolong the life of your deck, you should apply a protective finish every couple of years or so. Aside from enhancing the beauty of the wood or imparting an attractive color, a quality wood finish will slow the damaging effects of water and sunlight. Eventually, you may also need to make more drastic structural repairs as the wood ages and deteriorates. So, the tradeoff for building a beautiful deck is some degree of continual maintenance on your part. If you are diligent in these upkeep and repair efforts, your deck will last for decades and continue to be a functional, inviting feature of your home.

This chapter will introduce you to the common cleaning and finishing products that are available for preserving your deck. You'll learn how to apply finish to new wood and clean weathered or previously finished wood in preparation for refinishing. We'll also show you how to inspect your deck for rotten wood and walk you through the step-by-step process for replacing decking, joists, and rotten posts. The chapter concludes with ways to clean vinyl and other composite decking materials.

In this chapter:

- Cleaning, Sealing & Coloring a Deck
- Finishing a New Wood Deck
- Maintaining a Deck
- Repairing a Deck
- Cleaning Vinyl & Composite Decking

Cleaning, Sealing & Coloring a Deck

Whenever you finish or refinish your deck, there are three objectives: Cleaning the wood, protecting it, and creating the color you want. First, you need to clean the wood or remove a previous finish to prepare for applying new finish. Otherwise, the stain or sealer may not penetrate and bond properly. Second, a protective topcoat of stain or a sealer/preservative weatherizes the wood, limiting its ability to absorb water. Water absorption leads to rot and invites mildew and algae growth that can prematurely damage the finish. The topcoat also helps to block out ultraviolet sunlight, which will fade wood's natural color, age the finish, and dry out the wood until it cracks or splits. The third goal of finishing is the most obvious: staining allows you to change the wood color and either hide the wood grain or enhance it, depending on the product you choose.

If you think of finishing products in terms of cleaning, weatherizing, and coloring, you'll have an easier time choosing the right products for your deck-finishing project. Here is an overview of each category of finishing product.

After

Before

Deck Cleaner

If your deck's current finish has faded or the wood has algae or mildew growth, use a deck cleaner to remove these kinds of stubborn stains. Deck cleaner will restore gray, weathered wood back to its original color. It will remove general dirt and grime as well as grease spots left by grilling. If the deck is just dirty but not weathered, try using a dilute solution of ordinary dish soap, followed by a good scrubbing. Soap may be all the cleaning agent your deck really needs.

Waterproofing Sealer

Oil-based waterproofing sealers and wood finishes penetrate the wood, carrying silicone or wax additives that keep wood from absorbing water. Most sealers contain mildewcides and UV inhibitors for added protection. Use a waterproofing sealer when you want to preserve the natural color and grain of the wood. Some products will impart a bit of tinting and color, but generally a sealer will leave the wood looking natural when it dries. Unlike stains, sealers have little or no pigment to ward off fading from sunlight. You'll need to reapply a sealer every year or two to maintain UV protection.

Semi-transparent Stain

Semi-transparent stains offer similar protective qualities similar to waterproofing sealer, but with more pigment added to help the wood resist fading. The more obvious purpose of the pigment, however, is to color the wood or blend different wood tones without obscuring the grain pattern. These stains are oil-based and penetrating, but they do not form a film on the wood's surface. They're a better choice for decking, benches and horizontal surfaces than solid-color stains, because they won't peel. Plan to reapply every two to four years.

Solid-color Stain

Solid-color stain contains much more pigment than semi-transparent stain, and the formulation is closer to thinned paint than to stain. If you want to completely hide wood grain, a solid-color stain is the right choice for the job. It's a blend of oil and latex or latex only, so the stain forms a film on the wood surface instead of penetrating it. As long as the film doesn't peel or crack, it provides superior protection against both water and UV degradation. However, it doesn't stand up to foot traffic as well as oil-based stain. Solid-color stains can be blended in thousands of paint colors. The finish can last five years or more, but generally it will need to be stripped or sanded first before recoating. Avoid using solid-color stain on redwood or cedar. These woods have tannins and resins than can bleed through the stain and leave spots.

Finishing a New Wood Deck

Finish a deck with clear sealer-preservative or staining sealer. Sealer-preservatives protect wood from water and rot, and are often used on cedar or redwood because they preserve the original color of the wood. If you want the wood to look weathered, wait several months before applying sealer-preservative.

Staining sealers, sometimes called toners, are often applied to pressure-treated lumber to give it the look of redwood or cedar. Staining sealers are available in a variety of colors.

For best protection, use finishing products with an alkyd base. Apply fresh finish each year.

Tools & Materials ▶

Belt sander
Sandpaper
Shop vacuum
Pressure sprayer
Eye protection

Paint brush
Clear sealer-
   preservative or
   staining sealer

Tip ▶

Use an orbital sander to smooth out any rough areas before applying finish to decking boards, railings, or stair treads.

A hand-pump style sprayer is inexpensive and speeds up the finish application process.

Oil & Grease Stains: Oil and grease spots from barbecuing or tanning lotions should be cleaned immediately, before they dry. Use a household degreaser (such as an orange citrus cleaner), Simple Green, or ammonia and a scrub brush to remove the stain. Follow with soapy water and thorough rinsing.

Mold & Mildew: Use a diluted solution of household bleach and water or a deck cleaner with mildew and stain remover to kill off mold and mildew growth. A good preventive measure is to scrub and wash your deck at least once a season, especially in shady or damp areas where mold and mildew are likely to grow.

Berry & Wine Stains: Use a dilute solution of household bleach and water to spot-clean wine or berry stains from decking. Depending on the depth of the stain, you may not be able to remove it entirely, but generally these stains will fade over time.

Crayon & Marker Stains: If you have young kids, sooner or later crayon or marker stains are inevitable. The trick to removing them is using the correct solvent. Mineral spirits will remove crayon wax, and soapy water cleans up water-based marker stains. Use denatured alcohol (available at home centers) to remove dye-based, permanent markers.

Deck Materials & Tools

Constructing a deck requires a variety of building materials, and this chapter will introduce you to them. You'll need forms, concrete and gravel for making footings, treated posts and framing lumber for the deck's undercarriage, an assortment of connective hardware and fasteners, flashing supplies, decking and materials for building railings and stairs. Get ready to make some long shopping lists! You may also want to acquaint yourself with the deck-building section of your local home center before you start your deck project. That way, you'll be able to find what you need quickly and easily when you really need it.

If you're a seasoned do-it-yourselfer or woodworker, you may already own most of the hand and power tools you'll need for building a deck. You'll also need a few masonry tools. Be sure to review the specialty tools (pages 202 and 203) that you may want to rent for your deck project. They may save you considerable time and effort.

In this chapter:

- Footings & Structural Lumber
- Wood Decking
- Composite Decking
- Fasteners & Hardware
- Metal Connecting Hardware
- Screws & Nails
- Flashing
- Footing Forms
- Specialty Tools

Footings & Structural Lumber

Generally, pressure-treated lumber is the preferred choice for deck posts, beams, and joist framing. It offers good resistance to decay and insect infestation, it's widely available in most parts of the country and it's a cheaper alternative to other rot-resistant wood species such as cedar or redwood. Treated lumber is milled in 4 × 4, 4 × 6, and 6 × 6 sizes for posts. Larger dimensions are available by special order. You'll need 2× treated lumber for beams and joists. Joists are usually 2 × 8 or larger. If your deck is particularly large or designed with oversized spans, you may need to use engineered beams instead of building beams from treated lumber. Make sure your engineered beams are rated for exterior use.

Select the flattest structural lumber you can find, free of splits, checks, and large loose knots. To prevent warping, stack and store it in a dry place or cover it with a tarp until you need it. Check the grade stamps or the stapled tags on your pressure-treated posts; they should be approved to a level of .40 retention for ground contact.

Chemical Formulations of Pressure-treated Lumber ▸

As of January 1, 2004, the lumber industry voluntarily discontinued the use of chromated copper arsenate (CCA) treated lumber for consumer uses. This was done in conjunction with the Environmental Protection Agency in an effort to help reduce the exposure to arsenic, a known carcinogen. Two alternative chemical treatments are now used instead: alkaline copper quaternary (ACQ) and copper boron azole (CBA). Both ACQ and CBA provide wood with the same protection from decay and insect attack as CCA, however the treatments are more corrosive to metals. Make sure to choose fasteners and connective hardware that are approved for use with ACQ- and CCA-treated lumber.

Treated lumber is available in common nominal sizes for use as deck beams and joists. Choose the clearest, flattest boards you can find, free of checks and splits. Use the correct post size for the deck you are building: 4 × 4s and 4 × 6s are still acceptable for railing and stair construction, but they do not meet requirements for deck posts. You'll need 6 × 6 or larger lumber for this purpose.

Lumber for Building Decks

Engineered beams that are rated for exterior use are a sturdy alternative to beams made from 2× lumber. They may be required if you are building a large deck with expansive or unusual spans. Your building inspector will help you make this determination.

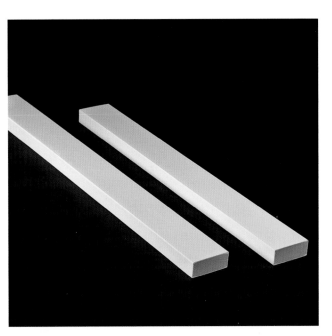

Composite lumber is growing in acceptance as the technology advances. While it is still not rated for most structural purposes, dimensional lumber made from composites is becoming available for lighter duty jobs, such as providing nailing surfaces for a screened-in porch.

Tip ▸

Seal cut edges of all lumber, including pressure-treated wood, by brushing on clear liquid sealer-preservative. Chemicals used in pressure treatment do not always penetrate completely. Sealer-preservative protects all types of wood from rot.

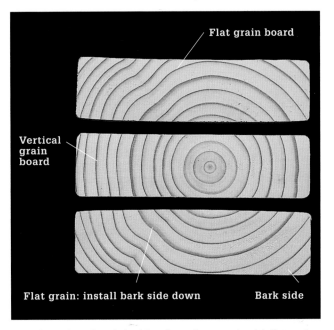

Check end grain of decking boards. Boards with flat grain tend to "cup," and can trap standing water if not installed properly. Research studies indicate that flat grain boards cup toward the bark side (not away from it, as was previously thought in the industry), and they should be installed so the bark side faces down.

Wood Decking

Wood decking continues to be the preferred choice over composite decking, primarily due to price. Pressure-treated decking, for instance, is still less than half the cost of synthetic decking. Aside from cost, wood has an inviting natural appeal. It's easy to work with and available everywhere. Although the perception of composite decking is changing as it grows in popularity, when you think about a deck, chances are you still imagine the surface covered in real wood.

The two most popular choices for wood decking are pressure-treated and cedar. Depending on where you live, you may have other options as well. Redwood may still be available if you live on the west coast, and cypress is common in the south. Redwood, cypress, and cedar are naturally resistant to decay and insect pests, which makes them excellent choices for decking. You can apply finish if you like, or leave them unfinished and they'll weather to a silvery gray color in a few years. If cost is less important than quality, you might consider covering your deck with mahogany or ipê, a South-American exotic sometimes called ironwood.

For pressure-treated or cedar decking, you'll have to select a thickness that works for your budget and design. One option is to use 2× lumber. It will span wider joist spacing without flexing, but generally 2× lumber is made from lower-grade material that may contain more natural defects. Another choice is to use 5/4 decking, pronounced "five quarter." Its thickness is closer to 1 inch and the edges are radiused to help minimize splinters. Often, 5/4 lumber is clearer than 2× lumber, but it's not as stiff. You may need to space your joists more closely with 5/4 decking. Either way, you can commonly find 2× or 5/4 decking in lengths up to 16 or even 20 ft. at most home centers.

Ipê

Cedar

Pressure-treated pine

Wood Decking

Both 2x and 5/4 lumber are suitable for use as decking. However, 5/4 will generally be of higher quality, and the radiused edges prevent splintering—an important consideration for bare feet or if you have young children.

If you hand-select each of your deck boards, look for pieces with vertical grain pattern (left in photo). They'll be less inclined to cup and warp than flat-grain lumber (right), but the wood tends to be significantly heavier.

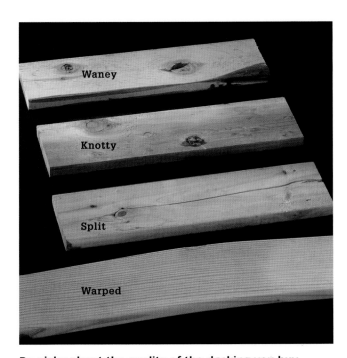

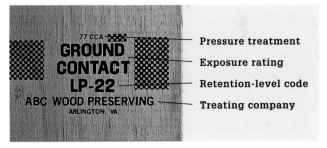

Pressure-treated lumber stamps list the type of preservative and the chemical retention level, as well as the exposure rating and the name and location of the treating company.

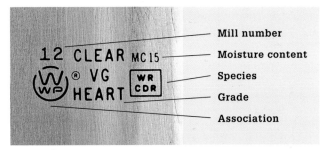

Be picky about the quality of the decking you buy. Natural defects in the wood could make the piece harder to install or deteriorate prematurely. Watch for soft pockets of sap in the wood. Sap will get sticky in warm weather, and the resin can bleed through wood finishes, leaving brown stains.

Cedar grade stamps list the mill number, moisture content, species, lumber grade, and membership association. Western red cedar (WRC) or incense cedar (INC) for decks should be heartwood (HEART) with a maximum moisture content of 15% (MC15).

Composite Decking

Composite decking has only been around for a few decades, but it's a compelling option to consider for your deck. Most forms of composite decking are made from a blend of post-consumer plastic waste and wood pulp or non-wood fibers. The plastic component—polyethylene or polypropylene—makes the material impervious to rotting, and insects don't like it. Unlike solid wood, it has no grain, so it won't splinter or crack, and there are no knots or natural defects to cut away. Other formulations of synthetic decking contain no wood at all. These are made from polyethylene, PVC, polystyrene or fiberglass blends. Composite decking comes with impressive warranties, which may last from 10 years to a lifetime, depending on the product. Some warranties are transferable from one homeowner to the next.

When composite lumber first hit the market, it didn't look anything like wood, and color choices were limited. Now, it's available in a range of wood textures and colors. Most products are non-toxic; easy to cut, drill, and fasten; and do not require finishing. Maintenance is usually limited to an occasional cleaning or spot removal. However, composite decking is more flexible than wood, so you may need to use closer joist spacing in your deck design. It's also heavier than wood and considerably more expensive.

Composites ▸

Composite materials blend together wood fibers and recycled plastics to create a rigid product that, unlike wood, will not rot, splinter, warp, or crack. Painting or staining is unnecessary. Like wood, these deck boards can be cut to size, using a circular saw with a large tooth blade.

PVC vinyl and plastic decking materials are shipped in kits that contain everything necessary to install the decking other than the deck screws. The kits are preordered to size, usually in multiples of the combined width of a deck board and the fasteners. The drawback of PVC vinyl decking is that it expands and contracts with freeze/thaw cycles.

Fiberglass reinforced plastic (FRP) decking will last a lifetime. Manufacturers claim that the material is three times as strong as wood and not affected by heat, sunlight, or severe weather. The decking is preordered to size but if necessary, it can be cut using a circular saw with a diamond-tip blade or masonry blade.

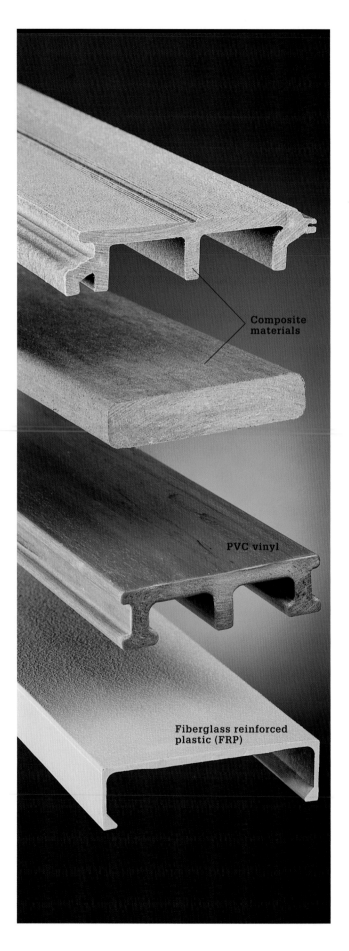

Composite materials

PVC vinyl

Fiberglass reinforced plastic (FRP)

Surface patterns for composite decking range from virtually no pattern to straight or cathedral wood grain styles. Pattern options will vary by product and manufacturer. Some simulated wood grains are quite convincing!

Composite decking colors cover the spectrum of wood tones, plus grays and white. The color is continuous throughout the material, but full exposure to sunlight may cause the surface color to fade.

While composite decking can be fastened down conventionally with screws, you may be able to use various edge-fastening systems instead to avoid driving screws through the board faces. For more on these options, see pages 109 to 117.

Composite and other nonwood decking often requires special fasteners that are designed to reduce "mushrooming" that occurs when the decking material bulges up around the screwhead. Pilot holes are recommended for some types as well.

Fasteners & Hardware

Certain structural connections of your deck will require the use of lag screws, through bolts and concrete anchors to withstand the heavy loads and sheer forces applied to a deck. Attaching ledger boards to your home's band joist, fastening beams to posts or anchoring posts to concrete footings are all areas where you'll need to step up to larger fasteners and anchors. Be sure to use hot-dipped galvanized or stainless-steel hardware to prevent rusting or corrosion from pressure-treating chemicals. Building codes require that you install a washer beneath the heads of lag screws or bolts and another washer before attaching nuts. Washers prevent fasteners from tearing through wood and secure hardware under stress.

Another fastening option to consider is high-strength epoxy, applied from a syringe. If you are fastening deck posts or ledger boards to cured concrete, the epoxy will bond threaded rod permanently in place without needing an additional metal anchor.

Here is an overview of the anchoring fasteners you may need for your project.

Galvanized or stainless steel lag bolts and washers are the correct fasteners for installing ledgers to the band joist of a house. You can also use them for making other wood-to-wood connections.

Anchoring Fasteners

Use ½"-diameter or larger through bolts, washers and nuts for fastening beams to posts or railing posts to joists. They should be galvanized or made of stainless steel for corrosion resistance.

J-bolts, embedded in the wet concrete of deck footings, provide a secure connection for attaching concrete footings to metal connecting hardware.

Wedge or sleeve anchors draw a wedge through a hollow sleeve, expanding it to form a tight fit in solid concrete. A nut and threaded end hold the ledger boards in place.

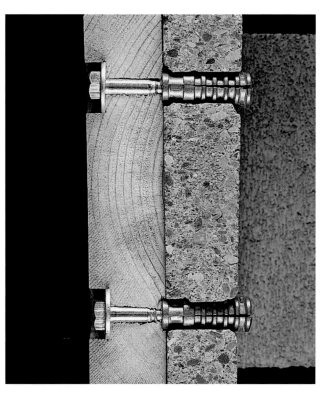

Soft metal shield anchors expand when lag screws are driven into them. They make suitable connections in either solid concrete or hollow block foundations.

A bolt driven through the foundation from the inside can be fitted with a washer and bolt to secure the ledger.

High strength epoxy and threaded rod are good options for attaching metal connecting hardware to concrete footings.

Metal Connecting Hardware

Sheet-metal connecting hardware comes in assorted shapes and styles. It is used to create strong wood-to-wood or wood-to-concrete joints quickly and easily. For instance, metal post anchors not only provide a simple way to attach posts and footings, but they also create space between the two surfaces so post ends stay dry. Joist hangers are a fast way to hang long, heavy joists accurately. Post beam caps, T-straps, and angled joist hangers are ideal solutions for building stacked joints or when space doesn't allow you access to drive screws or nails from behind the joint.

Make sure to buy hot-dipped galvanized or stainless steel connecting hardware. Some styles are designed for interior use only and do not have adequate corrosion protection. The product label should identify whether or not the hardware is suitable for pressure-treated wood and outdoor use. Use joist hanger nails made from the same material as the hardware.

Deck post ties fasten stair or railing posts to stringers or joists without through bolts. Hardware is manufactured in 2 × 4 and 4 × 4 size options.

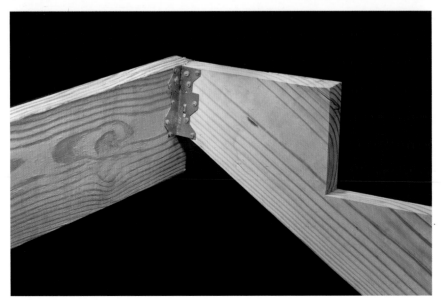

Framing anchors can be used to fasten rim joists together at corners or make other right-angle attachments, such as stair stringers to rim joists.

Hanger Hardware for Decks

Post anchors hold deck posts in place, and raise the base of the posts to help prevent water from entering end grain of wood.

Angle brackets help reinforce header and outside joists. Angle brackets are also used to attach stair stringers to the deck.

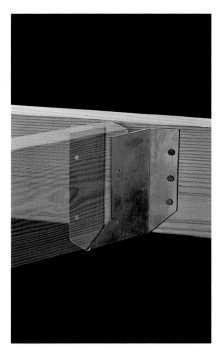

Joist hangers are used to attach joists to the ledger and header joist. Double hangers are used when decking patterns require a double-width joist.

Angled joist hangers are used to frame decks that have unusual angles or decking patterns.

Stair cleats support the treads of deck steps. Cleats are attached to stair stringers with ¼ × 1¼" galvanized lag screws.

(continued)

Post-beam caps secure beams on top of posts and are available in one-piece or adjustable styles.

H-fit rafter ties attach 2× joists or rafters to the top of a beam between beam ends.

Seismic ties attach 2× joists or rafters to the top of a beam at its ends.

Skewable joist hangers attach 2× lumber, such as stair stringers, to the face of framing at an adjustable angle.

Skewable angle brackets reinforce framing connections at angles other than 90 degrees or at beam ends where 45-degree joist hangers won't fit.

Direct bearing footing connectors attach beams directly to footings on low profile decks.

T-straps reinforce the connection between beam and post, particularly on long beams requiring spliced construction. Local building codes may also allow their use in place of post caps.

Strapping plates, also known as nailing plates or mending plates, are useful for a variety of reinforcement applications.

Screws & Nails

When you attach the beams and joists of your deck, and probably the decking as well, you'll need a collection of screws and/or nails to get these jobs done. It may not seem like screw and nail technology would change all that much, but in fact there are many new products available for making these essential connections. If you build your deck from pressure-treated lumber, be sure to use stainless, hot-dipped galvanized, or specially coated fasteners that are approved for use with the more corrosive ACQ and CBA wood preservatives. Spiral or ring-shank nails will offer better holding power than smooth nails. Use screws with auger tips and self-drilling heads to avoid drilling pilot holes. Some screws are specially designed for installing composite decking. They have a variable thread pattern that keeps the heads from mushrooming the surrounding material when driven flush.

If you are building a large deck, consider using a pneumatic nailer with collated nails instead of hand nailing. Collated screws are a faster way to lay deck boards than driving each screw individually. Here's an overview of your fastener options.

Whether you are fastening framing together or installing deck boards, your screw options include stainless steel or galvanized. You can also buy screws with colored coatings formulated to resist corrosion from pressure-treated wood. Stainless or coated screws will prevent black staining that can occur on cedar.

Screws & Nails for Decks

Use stainless steel or hot-dipped galvanized framing nails to assemble beams and joists. Install metal connector hardware with 8d or 10d hot-dipped galvanized metal connector nails.

For large deck projects, galvanized pneumatic nails or coated, collated screws are a faster way to fasten framing and decking than driving each nail or screw by hand.

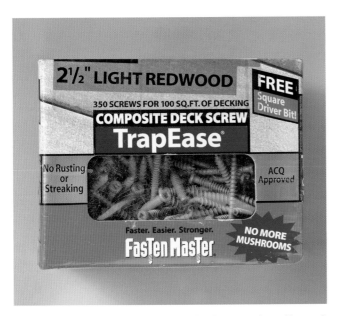

Make sure your fasteners will resist the corrosive effects of today's pressure-treating chemicals. Fastener manufacturers will usually provide this information on the product label.

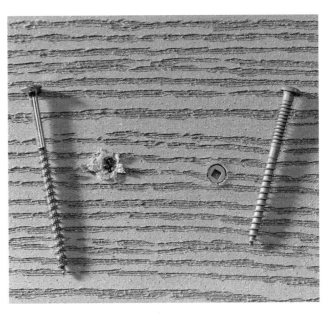

One drawback to composite decking is that it tends to "mushroom" around screwheads unless the screws are driven into pilot holes. Some screws are designed with undercut heads and a variable pitch pattern to avoid this problem.

If you'd prefer not to see screwheads in your decking but still want to drive them from the surface, you can buy screws with snap-off heads. A special tool breaks the head off after the screw is driven. The resulting hole is much smaller than a screwhead.

Choose your nails and screws carefully. Screws with "bright" or black-oxide coatings and uncoated nails will not stand up to exterior use or pressure-treating chemicals. Fasteners are as crucial to your deck's long-term durability as the quality of the framing lumber or decking.

Flashing

Building codes require that a deck's ledger board be attached directly to wall sheathing and house framing. If your home is sided, you'll need to remove the siding in the ledger board area before attaching the ledger to the house. Be sure to install 15# or 30# building paper or self-sealing, adhesive backed membrane behind the ledger to prevent moisture damage. Rotting in the area behind the ledger is one of the leading causes of premature deck deterioration. Flashing is particularly important if there's no housewrap behind the siding. Once the ledger is in place, cap it with a piece of galvanized Z-flashing, tucked behind the siding, for added protection.

Although building code doesn't require it, you may also want to wrap the tops of beams and posts with self-sealing membrane to keep these areas dry and rot-free. Ledger flashing, self-sealing membrane and building paper are available at most home centers and lumberyards. They're little details that can make a big difference to the longevity of your deck.

Building felt, also called building paper, is used behind house siding materials. Use it to replace felt damaged during a ledger installation. Ledger flashing, or Z-flashing, prevents moisture damage behind the deck ledger. Self-sealing membrane provides extra protection from moisture in damp climates or in areas where there is snow accumulation. It can be used over flashing or on top of beams and posts (see below), and it self-seals around nails or screws that pierce it.

To apply self-sealing membrane, cut a piece to size and position it over the application area. Starting at one end, begin removing the thin plastic backing that protects the adhesive. Firmly press the membrane in place as you remove the backing, working along the installation area. To install long pieces of membrane, enlist the aid of a helper.

Install self-sealing membrane behind the ledger as extra protection from moisture. Apply the membrane over the house wrap or building felt, using the same method shown at left.

Footing Forms

Footing forms, which are also called piers, anchor a deck to the ground and create a stable foundation for the posts. They transfer the weight of the deck into the soil and prevent it from heaving upward in climates where the ground freezes. Generally, footings are made from long, hollow tubes of fiber-reinforced paper in several diameters. Once a tube footing is set into the ground below the frostline, you backfill around the outside with soil, tamp it down firmly, and fill with concrete. Metal connective hardware imbedded in the concrete will attach the footings permanently to the deck posts.

For soils that have a poor bearing capacity, or if you are building a particularly large deck, you can also buy plastic footing tubes with flared bases that bear heavier loads. Or, you can attach a flared footing to the bottom of a conventional tube. For low-profile decks that aren't attached to a house, you may be able to use pre-cast concrete footings instead of buried piers. These precut footings simply rest on the surface of the soil.

Lumberyards and building centers will stock hollow footing forms in various diameters. The diameter you need will depend on the size and weight of your deck. Your building official will help you determine the correct size when you apply for a building permit.

Pre-cast concrete footings are usually acceptable for building low-profile, freestanding decks. Notches on top of the pier are designed to hold joists without fasteners or other hardware.

Cut away for clarity

When building heavy decks or placing footings in unstable, loose soil, you may need to use piers with flared footings. Some styles are molded in one piece, or you can attach a flared footing to a conventional footing form with screws.

Specialty Tools

A big deck project can be labor-intensive and time consuming. Certain specialized tools, such a power auger, hammer drill or collated screw gun, can speed tasks along and save you some of the sweat equity involved. But, these tools can be expensive, and they're hard to justify buying unless you plan to use them often. Renting them may be a better option. A wide assortment of tools, including the ones on these pages, are available at rental centers at a reasonable cost. Renting gives you an opportunity to try a tool that you're considering buying or use and return a tool you would never consider buying.

A collated screwgun speeds up the process of fastening decking to joists, and it can save wear and tear on your knees. These tools accept strips of exterior screws, and an advancing mechanism allows you to drive them one after the next without stopping. An adjustable clutch prevents the screws from being overdriven.

A laser level shines a continuous level line in a 360° plane. It's useful for striking off uniform post heights without measuring. Deck platforms should be flat and level in all directions. Posts should be plumb and located squarely on their footings. In order to achieve level and plumb, you'll probably need more than a carpenter's level in your tool collection. Consider buying a post speed level and a laser level. Post-speed levels fasten in place with a rubber band and have three spirit levels to help you adjust posts quickly and accurately. They're handy for setting both deck and fence posts.

Hammer drills combine the usual rotary action with forward motion, similar to a tiny jackhammer. They make it much easier to drill large pilot holes in concrete or block walls for installing ledger board anchors.

If you have more than a few holes to dig for your deck footings, especially when they're deep, rent a power auger. Both one-person and two-person models are available. A gas-powered engine drives the auger to excavate these holes quickly.

Cordless impact drivers can make quick work of laborious tasks like driving lag screws. Because they have a percussive motion as well as high-torque spinning motion, they leverage two forces at once. They are excellent for driving lag screws as well as deck screws.

Tools for straightening deck boards are relatively inexpensive and can quickly pay for themselves by allowing you to install badly bowed boards.

CUSTOM DECK
PROJECTS

A Deck for Entertaining

Outdoor entertaining on a deck often involves preparing a meal. If the menu is just burgers and hot dogs, most of that food prep takes place at the grill. But even the simplest fare still involves those inevitable trips back and forth to the kitchen to toss a salad, warm up a side dish or replenish the cold drinks. More complex meals will keep the chef in the kitchen even longer—and that means less time spent out on the deck with family and friends. Wouldn't it be great if you could bring the kitchen to the deck to take care of more—or even all—of those food prep tasks?

A decade or so ago, outdoor kitchens were still more fantasy than reality, but that's no longer the case.

Today, Americans are increasingly seeing their decks as important outdoor entertainment areas, and not just places to park the patio table and grill. An assortment of custom grills, outdoor appliances, and storage cabinets can help you transform your deck into a fully functional kitchen. These appliances are UL-listed, so your kitchen doesn't have to be located in a covered porch or tucked under a roof. You can cook and prepare right where you serve. Outdoor appliances are generally more expensive than their indoor cousins, but if outdoor entertaining is an important part of your lifestyle, you can now enjoy it more fully than ever before and without compromise.

Imagine the dinner parties you could host if your deck had a fully functional outdoor kitchen! It's a relatively new trend in outdoor entertaining that continues to grow in popularity. These days, there are outdoor appliances to suit most kitchen tasks.

Whether you use your deck for intimate outdoor dining, boisterous parties, or quiet conversation, decks provide an ideal way to extend your home's livable space into the outdoors.

A sturdy outdoor patio table and chairs, made of suitable exterior-rated wood or metal, is a beneficial improvement to any deck. Tables that accept large shade umbrellas are even more practical, especially if your deck is located in a sunny spot.

A high-end outdoor kitchen with stainless steel appliances and solid wood cabinetry leaves no question that this deck owner is serious about food.

Outdoor Appliances

For years, better quality grills have included a sideburner and second grate to keep food warm. Now, you can purchase expansive grilling stations that may include dedicated infrared warming drawers, storage cabinets and drawers, insulated cubbies for ice, and extended serving counters. They're a relatively affordable way to take your grilling and food preparation tasks to the next level, and you can buy these units at most home centers.

Self-contained grilling stations are just one of many appliance options to choose from. For more culinary convenience, you can also buy outdoor-rated ovens, multi-burner rangetops and refrigerators, ice makers, and beverage coolers from a number of reputable manufacturers. Ovens and rangetops are heated by either propane or natural gas, depending on the model. They're designed as modular components that fit into a bank of cabinets or a custom-built kitchen island. Outdoor refrigerators are relatively compact and nest under a countertop where they can be at least partially sheltered from the elements. They range in capacity from around 3 to 6 cubic feet. Outdoor sinks, wet bars, and dedicated food prep stations are other options you might consider adding to your deck kitchen.

A variety of outdoor kitchen appliances, such as refrigerators, ice makers, and wine coolers, can help keep food and drinks cold no matter how hot the day may be.

Custom barbecue islands can be configured in lots of different ways to suit your space and food prep needs. The primary appliance is generally a gas grill with a cabinet underneath for storing the LP tank. A bank of drawers provides handy places to keep grilling tools and other cooking utensils or spices.

A warming drawer outfitted in your barbecue island can help you stage various dinner items while you grill the main course. Some prefabricated barbecue islands include a warming drawer.

This self-contained beer keg cooler will keep your favorite brew cold on the hottest summer day and for as long as the party lasts. All it takes is an electrical outlet.

Consider adding a plumbed sink to your outdoor kitchen. It will make food prep and clean-up much easier. Be sure to check with local building codes concerning running hot and cold supply lines or installing an appropriate drain.

If your barbecue grill isn't equipped with a side burner, it's an essential feature you'll want to add to your outdoor kitchen. Side burners are available as independent accessories that can be built into a kitchen island or bank of cabinets.

Cabinets & Countertops

Once you step beyond a one-piece grilling station, you'll need to store a stove, refrigerator or other appliances in a system of cabinets or an island base of some kind. This could be as simple as an enclosed framework with a countertop, or it can be as elaborate as you like. Chances are, you'll want to include a few storage cabinets and drawers to keep utensils, cookware and other supplies close at hand. Some cabinet manufacturers offer weather-resistant cabinets made from teak, cypress, mahogany, or other exterior woods. They're available as modular components that can be mixed and matched like other cabinetry. Polyethylene, marine-grade polymer or stainless steel cabinets are more options to consider: they're corrosion-resistant, waterproof and hypoallergenic. It's a good idea to buy your appliances first, then design an island or bank of cabinets that will fit what you own.

A variety of countertop materials could make a durable and attractive serving surface for your kitchen. Porcelain tile is weather-resistant and affordable, and it's manufactured in virtually any style and color you can dream of. You could choose a fabricated countertop made of stainless steel, soapstone, granite, or marble. Or, build your counter from a piece of tempered glass. If your deck kitchen will be sheltered under an awning or roof, solid-surface material is also good choice. However, the polymer blends that make up solid-surface materials aren't formulated to be UV stable, and they could deteriorate over time.

If you build your own countertop, be sure to start with a substrate layer of cement backer board if you use grouted tile or other permeable material. It will prevent water from seeping through to appliances or into storage cabinets.

Building an Island Base

For handy do-it-yourselfers, designing a weatherproof kitchen island can offer a hearty challenge and an excellent chance to explore some new building materials. Start with a framework of pressure-treated or cedar lumber, and sheathe it with waterproof cement backer board. Then, cover the exposed surfaces with patio tile, stucco, veneered stone or brick. Or,

use exterior plywood as the substrate for your island framework, then follow with vinyl, fiber cement or cedar lap siding to match the siding of your house. You could even use composite decking to sheathe your kitchen island or grilling station so it visually ties it in with your deck's design. Or, wrap the outside in sheets of stainless steel or aluminum for a sleek, modern look.

Build or Hire? ▶

Depending on where you live, you might be able to hire a contractor to design and build the countertop, base and cabinets for your deck appliances. However, given that deck kitchens are still a relatively new concept, you may need to carry out these projects on your own. Companies that sell outdoor appliances and cabinetry may be able to help you design your outdoor deck kitchen. You can also find grilling station and island project designs in outdoor kitchen design books.

Keep in mind that you may need to run a natural gas line and several ground-fault protected outlets to the kitchen. If you decide to include a functional sink in your design, you'll need at least one potable water line and possibly a sanitary drain that empties into a dry well or your home's plumbing system. Be sure to install these utilities so that they conform to the building codes in your area. The proper course of action is to apply for the appropriate utility permits and have the work inspected. If you are in doubt of your skills with running gas lines or wiring electrical receptacles, have this work performed by a licensed plumber and electrician.

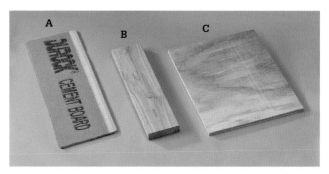

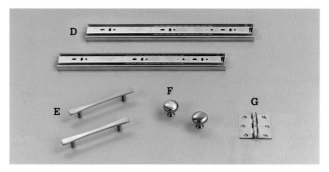

You'll want to expand the storage capabilities of your deck kitchen by including a variety of cabinets. Exterior-grade cabinets are made with durable polymers, rot-resistant woods, or stainless steel, and they are available in a range of sizes and styles to suit your needs.

Choose water-resistant building materials for the structural and sheathing components of your island. Cement board (A), outdoor woods like cedar or redwood (B), and exterior-rated plywood (C) are all suitable home-center options. For cabinets, choose corrosion-resistant drawer slides (D), drawer hardware (E, F), and hinges (G).

If you're a competent woodworker, consider building custom cabinets to outfit your deck kitchen rather than buying them. Then, make them from the same wood as your other patio furniture or decking so they blend into your deck scheme perfectly.

Soapstone is a moderately hard, natural material that works well for exterior countertop applications. The stone is semi-porous, so it should be periodically sealed if it's exposed to the elements. Sealing helps maintain water resistance.

Granite is an excellent countertop material. It's much harder than soapstone and available in many natural colors and surface textures. Generally, it's also more expensive than soapstone.

Concrete is more affordable than natural stone, and it can be tinted in a wide range of colors or mixed with other aggregates to add texture and visual interest. Another benefit to concrete is that it can be poured to suit any shape of countertop you may need.

Grouted patio tile will also work well for an outdoor kitchen countertop. It's inexpensive, easy to install without special skills and comes in many sizes, colors, and styles. You'll need to seal the grout periodically if the countertop is exposed to the elements or has a sink.

Is Your Deck Well Suited for a Kitchen? ▸

A deck kitchen may sound like an intriguing notion, but think carefully about the ramifications of dedicating part of your deck to this purpose. You'll need a certain amount of counter space for preparing food and staging it for cooking or storing it while you cook. Do you want to reserve a portion of the counter area for dining, or will that take place at a separate patio table? Are your home's utilities close enough to the deck to make gas lines or plumbing convenient to run? Will a kitchen island, patio table, and other deck furniture all fit comfortably on your deck without making the space feel crowded? As you begin to plan your outdoor kitchen, it may help to use masking tape, pieces of plywood, or cardboard boxes to lay out a space for your kitchen. This will help you visualize how the size of the kitchen would impact the rest of your deck. Ultimately, an outdoor kitchen should enhance your outdoor entertaining options and make your deck more useful, not overwhelm it.

A Deck for Livability

Decks are significant investments, so you should try to use yours as much as possible. Don't let those dog days of summer, a chilly fall afternoon, or sundown cut your deck enjoyment short. A few carefully chosen accessories can improve creature comforts and get you back out on the deck earlier each spring or extend your entertaining later into the year. If you are a serious audiophile or sports fan, an outdoor sound system or television might be just what you need to spend more time outdoors and on the deck. Manufacturers of lighting and deck accessories are continually expanding their product lines. Visit their websites or attend a home and garden show to get a better taste of what's new and exciting in deck accessories. The selection of products on display at your local home center are just the tip of the iceberg.

The following pages cover a variety of deck accessories that will make your deck a more practical and vital part of your leisure lifestyle.

The "livability" of your deck is a somewhat intangible quality rooted in form, function, and the natural conditions that impact it. Shade and sunlight, location and furniture, amenities like hot tubs or kitchens, provisions for privacy, and the way in which the desk's space is laid out all influence how often and well you'll use it.

An outdoor kitchen with ample counterspace for food preparation and serving as well as seating for casual dining will help to make it a hard-working feature of your deck.

If your deck will receive lots of sunshine or you are located in a southern climate, consider adding a retractable sunshade for those really hot days. Or, cover a portion of your deck with a fixed awning.

Deck living can extend well into the fall or even the winter if you include a heat source on your deck. A permanent outdoor fireplace like the one shown here is only one option. You can also buy free-standing or fixed radiant heaters that burn propane or natural gas. Or, use a chiminea or a raised firepit to keep folks warm when there's a chill.

Broad, sturdy benches will invite relaxation, especially if they're located on a portion of your deck that receives some shade. Depending on the height of your deck, fixed benches could even take the place of railings.

Recessed stair lighting clearly serves a safety function, but it also offers a cheery welcome for evening visitors. It should be combined with other light sources to create a pleasant, well-lit area.

Railing posts are another good spot for adding accent lighting. You can buy low-voltage post cap lights in various styles to take your deck lighting "to the next level," so to speak. It's a custom touch that will impress.

There are lots of options for deck lighting fixtures. These low-standing, pier-styled lights suggest a nautical theme and would be ideal for a deck located near a lake or other water feature.

An arbor provides a pleasant filter of sun and shade. It's also a great place to plant vining leafy plants, which will eventually cover the top and contribute even more natural shade. Wooden arbors make great DIY projects, whether you install one when your deck first goes up or any time you want to add a custom touch.

Your deck will be a more inviting place to gather and spend time if you break up the space with lots of interesting details. Raised planters, benches, and a unique railing style all contribute a sense of craftsmanship and purpose to a well-planned deck.

Exterior-rated audio systems and even waterproof televisions can help transform your deck into an outdoor living room. Add a few comfy patio chairs and occasional tables, and you may be surprised how much more time you spend on the deck than in the living room!

These white lattice railings and attached arbor give this deck a bright, friendly atmosphere. Thanks to ample shading, a long, cushioned bench certainly makes a perfect spot for reading or even an afternoon nap on a lazy day.

A Deck with Power

The wiring installation shown on the following pages provides step-by-step instructions for installing light fixtures and power receptacles on a deck. These instructions are based on the National Electrical Code (NEC), which stipulates minimum standards for outdoor wiring materials. But because climate and soil conditions vary from region to region, always check with your local building and electrical codes for additional restrictions in your area. For example, some codes require that all underground cables be protected with conduit, even though the NEC allows UF cable to be buried without protection at the proper depths.

Note: This project requires general knowledge of electrical materials and techniques beyond the specific instructions shown here. Make certain you know how to do this work before attempting this project.

Check for underground utilities when planning trenches for underground cable runs. Avoid lawn sprinkler pipes, and consult your electric utility office, phone company, gas and water department, and cable television vendor for the exact locations of underground utility lines. Many utility companies send field representatives to accurately locate dangerous underground hazards.

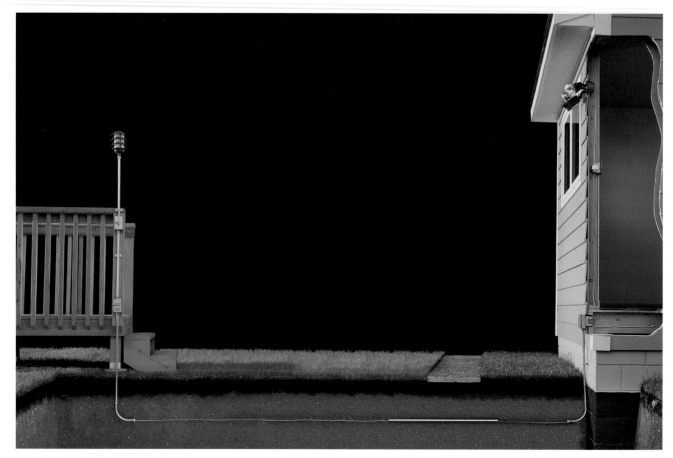

Running underground cable to supply power to your deck is a relatively simple wiring job that offers high payback in deck enjoyment for your family.

How to Wire a Deck

PLAN THE CIRCUIT

Visit your electrical inspector to check local code requirements for outdoor wiring and to obtain a permit for your project. Because outdoor wiring is exposed to the elements, it requires the use of special weatherproof materials, including UF cable, rigid metal or schedule 40 PVC plastic conduit, weatherproof electrical boxes and fittings. Some local codes allow either rigid metal or PVC plastic, while others allow only metal.

For most homes, an outdoor circuit for a deck is a modest power user. Adding a new 15-amp, 120-volt circuit provides enough power for most needs. However, if your circuit will include more than three large light fixtures (each rated for 300 watts or more) or more than four receptacles, plan to install a 20-amp, 120-volt circuit.

Consider the circuit length when choosing cable sizes for the deck circuit. In very long circuits, normal wire resistance leads to a substantial drop in voltage. If your circuit extends more than 50 feet, use cable wire that is one gauge larger to reduce the voltage drop. For example, a 15-amp circuit that extends more than 50 feet should be wired with 12-gauge wire instead of the usual 14-gauge.

Plan to bury UF cables 12" deep if the wires are protected by a GFCI and the circuit is no larger than 20 amps. Bury cable at least 18" deep if the circuit is not protected by a GFCI or if it is larger than 20 amps **(photo 1)**.

Prevent shock by making sure all outdoor receptacles are GFCI protected. A single GFCI receptacle can be wired to protect other fixtures on the circuit. Outdoor receptacles should be at least 12" above ground level and enclosed in weatherproof electrical boxes with watertight covers **(photo 2)**.

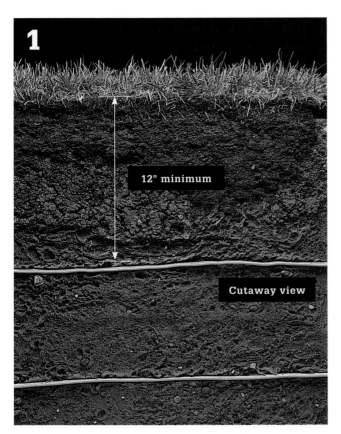

Bury UF cables 12" deep if the wires are protected by a GFCI and the circuit is no larger than 20 amps. Bury cable at least 18" deep if the circuit is not protected by a GFCI, or if it is larger than 20 amps.

Install GFCI receptacles in weatherproof electrical boxes at least 1 ft.—and no more than 6½ ft.—above ground level.

DIG TRENCHES

When laying underground cables, save time and minimize lawn damage by digging trenches as narrow as possible. Plan the circuit to reduce the length of cable runs. If your soil is sandy, or very hard and dry, water the ground thoroughly before you begin digging.

Mark the outline of the trenches with wooden stakes and string.

Cut two 18"-wide strips of plastic, and place one strip on each side of the trench outline.

Remove blocks of sod from the trench outline, using a shovel. Cut sod 2" to 3" deep to keep roots intact. Place the sod on one of the plastic strips and keep it moist but not wet. It should be replaced within two or three days, otherwise the grass underneath the plastic may die.

Dig the trenches to the depth required by your local code. Heap the dirt onto the second strip of plastic (**photo 3**).

To run cable under a sidewalk, cut a length of metal conduit about 12" longer than the width of sidewalk, then flatten one end of the conduit to form a sharp tip. Drive the conduit through the soil under the sidewalk, using a ball-peen or masonry hammer and a wood block to prevent damage to the pipe (**photo 4**). Cut off the ends of the conduit with a hacksaw, leaving about 2" of exposed conduit on each side. Attach a compression fitting and plastic bushing to each end of the conduit. The plastic fittings will prevent the sharp edges of the conduit from damaging the cable sheathing.

If the trenches must be left unattended during the project, temporarily cover them with scrap plywood to prevent accidents.

INSTALL BOXES & CONDUIT

Outline the GFCI receptacle box on the exterior wall of the house. First drill pilot holes at the corners of the box outline, then use a piece of stiff wire to probe the wall for electrical wires or plumbing pipes. Complete the cutout with a jigsaw or reciprocating saw. *Masonry variation:* To make cutouts in masonry, drill a line of holes inside the box outline, using a masonry bit, then remove the waste material with a masonry chisel and ball-peen hammer.

Install nm cable from the circuit breaker panel to the GFCI cutout. Allow an extra 24" of cable at the panel end and an extra 12" at the GFCI end. Attach the cable to framing members with cable staples. Strip 10" of outer sheathing from the GFCI end of the cable and ¾" of insulation from each wire.

Outline trench locations with stakes and string, then dig the trenches to the depths required by your local code.

Drive conduit beneath sidewalks and other obstacles, using a block of wood and a hammer.

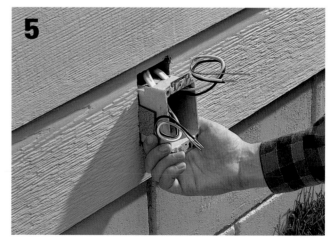

Route cables into the GFCI box, push the box into the cutout, then tighten the mounting screws until the box is secure.

Open one knockout for each cable that will enter the GFCI box. Insert the cables so at least ¼" of sheathing reaches into the box. Push the box into the cutout and tighten the mounting screw until the bracket draws the plaster ears tight against the wall (**photo 5**).

Position a foam gasket over the GFCI box, then attach an extension ring to the box, using the mounting screws included with the extension ring. Seal any gaps around the extension ring with silicone caulk.

Measure and cut a length of IMC conduit to reach from the bottom of the extension ring to a point about 4" from the bottom of the trench. Attach the conduit to the extension ring using a compression fitting (**photo 6**). Anchor the conduit to the wall with a pipe strap and masonry screws. Or use masonry anchors and pan-head screws. Drill pilot holes for the anchors, using a masonry drill bit.

Attach compression fittings to the ends of the metal sweep fitting, then attach the sweep fitting to the end of the conduit. Screw a plastic bushing onto the exposed fitting end of the sweep to keep the metal edges from damaging the cable.

Attach mounting ears to the back of a weatherproof receptacle box, then attach the box to the deck frame by driving galvanized screws through the ears and into the post.

Measure and cut a length of IMC conduit to reach from the bottom of the receptacle box to a point about 4" from the bottom of the trench. Attach the conduit to the box with a compression fitting. Attach a sweep fitting and plastic bushing to the bottom of the conduit, using compression fittings (**photo 7**).

Cut a length of IMC conduit to reach from the top of the receptacle box to the switch box location. Attach the conduit to the receptacle box with a compression fitting. Anchor the conduit to the deck frame with pipe straps.

Attach mounting ears to the back of the switch box, then loosely attach the box to the conduit with a compression fitting. Anchor the box to the deck frame by driving galvanized screws through the ears and into the wood. Tighten the compression fitting with a wrench. Measure and cut a short length of IMC conduit to reach from the top of the switch box to the deck light location. Attach the conduit with a compression fitting (**photo 8**).

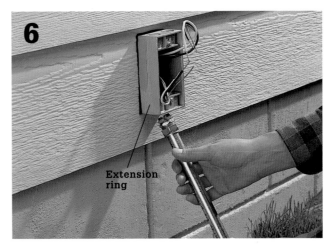

At the house, install conduit so it extends from the bottom of the extension ring to 4" from the bottom of the trench.

At the deck, attach conduit to the receptacle box so it extends from the bottom of the box to 4" from the bottom of the trench.

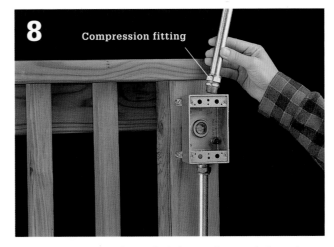

Attach conduit to the switch box so it extends from the box to the deck light location, using a compression fitting.

INSTALL THE CABLE

Measure and cut all UF cables, allowing an extra 12" at each box. At each end of the cable, use a utility knife to pare away about 3" of outer sheathing, leaving the inner wires exposed.

Feed a fish tape down through the conduit from the GFCI box. Hook the wires at one end of the cable through the loop in the fish tape, then wrap electrical tape around the wires up to the sheathing. Carefully pull the cable through the conduit (**photo 9**).

Lay the cable along the bottom of the trench, making sure it is not twisted. Where cable runs under a sidewalk, use the fish tape to pull it through the conduit.

Use the fish tape to pull the end of the cable up through the conduit to the deck receptacle box at the opposite end of the trench (**photo 10**). Remove the cable from the fish tape.

Cut away the electrical tape at each end of the cable, then clip away the bent wires. Bend back one of the wires in the cable, and grip it with needlenose pliers. Grip the cable with another pliers, then pull back on the wire, splitting the sheathing and exposing about 10" of wire. Repeat with the remaining wires, then cut off excess sheathing with a utility knife. Strip ¾" of insulation from the end of each wire, using a combination tool.

Measure, cut, and install a cable from the deck receptacle box to the outdoor switch box, using the fish tape. Strip 10" of sheathing from each end of the cable, then strip ¾" of insulation from the end of each wire, using a combination tool.

Attach a grounding pigtail to the back of each metal box and extension ring. Join all grounding wires with a wire connector. Tuck the wires inside the boxes, and temporarily attach the weatherproof coverplates until the inspector arrives for the rough-in inspection (**photo 11**).

CONNECT THE RECEPTACLES

At the GFCI receptacle, connect the black feed wire from the power source to the brass terminal marked "line". Connect the white feed wire from the power source to the silver screw terminal marked "line".

Attach the short white pigtail wire to the silver screw terminal marked "load", and attach a short black pigtail wire to the brass screw terminal marked "load".

Connect the black pigtail wire to all the remaining black circuit wires, using a wire connector. Connect the white pigtail wire to the remaining white circuit wires.

At the house, use fish tape to pull cable through the conduit and into the GFCI box.

At the deck, use the fish tape to pull cable through the conduit and into the receptacle box and switch box.

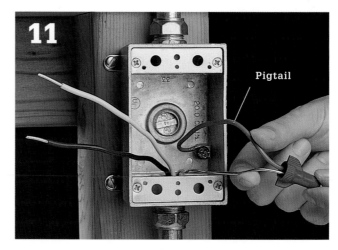

Pigtail

Connect a grounding pigtail to each metal box and extension ring and join all grounding wires with the pigtail. Install the coverplates for the rough-in inspection.

Attach a grounding pigtail to the grounding screw on the GFCI. Join the grounding pigtail to the bare copper grounding wires, using a wire connector (**photo 12**).

Carefully tuck the wires into the box. Mount the GFCI, then fit a foam gasket over the box and attach the weatherproof coverplate.

At each remaining receptacle in your deck circuit, connect the black circuit wires to the brass screw terminals on the receptacle. Connect the white circuit wires to the silver screw terminals on the receptacle. Attach a grounding pigtail to the grounding screw on the receptacle, then join all grounding wires with a wire connector.

Carefully tuck all wires into the box, and attach the receptacle to the box, using the mounting screws. Fit a foam gasket over the box, and attach the weatherproof coverplate.

CONNECT THE DECORATIVE LIGHT FIXTURES

Thread the wire leads of the light fixture through a threaded compression fitting. Screw the union onto the base of the light fixture (**photo 13**).

Feed the wire leads through the conduit and into the switch box. Slide the light fixture onto the conduit, and tighten the compression fitting.

CONNECT THE SWITCH

Switches for outdoor use have weatherproof coverplates with built-in toggle levers. The lever operates a single-pole switch mounted to the inside of the coverplate.

Connect the black circuit wire to one of the screw terminals on the switch, and connect the black wire lead from the light fixture to the other screw terminal.

Connect the black wire lead to one screw terminal on the switch, and connect the white wire lead to the white circuit wire (**photo 14**). Use a wire connector to join the grounding wires.

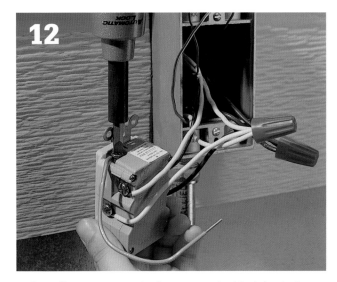

To install a GFCI receptacle, connect the black feed wire from the power source to the brass screw terminal (line), and the white feed wire to the silver screw terminal (line). Use pigtails and wire connectors to connect the remaining black circuit wires to the brass screw terminal (load), the white circuit wires to the silver screw terminal (load), and the green or copper wires to the grounding screw.

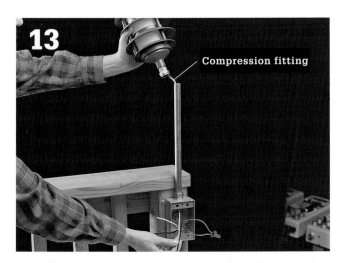

Feed the wire leads through the conduit into the switch box, then attach the light fixture using a compression fitting.

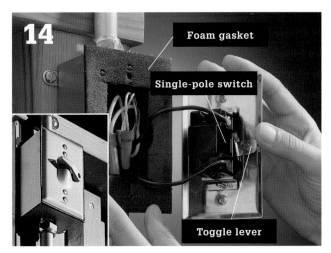

To install a weatherproof switch, connect the black circuit wire to one of the screw terminals on the switch, and the black wire lead from the fixture to the other screw terminal. Use wire connectors to join the white circuit wires and the grounding wires.

How to Install Low-voltage Step Lights

Low-voltage recessed lights are great for decks. Installed inconspicuously in the deck boards, they provide accent lighting for plant boxes or pathway lighting for stairs.

CUT THE HOLES FOR THE FIXTURES

Use the template or trace the bottom of the fixture onto the treads to mark a hole for each light. Center the fixture on the tread, 1 to 2" from the edge (the hole will center on the gap between the 2 × 6s on most deck stairs).

Drill holes at the corners, then cut the holes with a jigsaw (**photo 1**).

Test the fixtures to be sure they will fit (they should fit snugly), and adjust the holes as necessary.

RUN CABLE FOR THE FIXTURES

Run cable to the stairs from an existing low-voltage system or from a new transformer. Drill a hole in the bottom riser if necessary, and snake the cable under the stairs along the inside edge.

Pull a loop of cable through each of the holes for the fixtures and temporarily secure it to the tread with tape (**photo 2**).

WIRE THE FIXTURE

At the middle of the first loop of cable in the series, separate 3 to 4" of the two conductors in the cable by slicing down the center.

Strip about 2" of insulation off of each wire. Cut the wire in the center of the stripped section, and twist the two ends and the end of one of the fixture wires into an outdoor wire connector (**photo 3**). Secure the connection with electrical tape.

Repeat with the other fixture wire and the other circuit wire.

Tuck the wires back into the hole, and place the fixture into the hole.

Test each fixture before installing the next one.

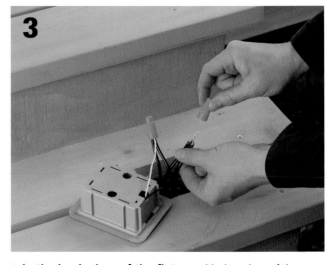

Mark the fixture location, then cut the holes using a jigsaw.

Run the cable from an existing low-voltage system or from a new transformer to the stair location.

Join the lead wires of the fixture with the wires of the low-voltage cable using outdoor wire connectors.

How to Install Low-voltage Railing Lights

Rope light is thin, flexible clear tubing with tiny light bulbs embedded every few inches along its length. Most rope lights are meant to plug into a receptacle and use household current. While this is all right for indoor decorating, it limits their use outdoors. Low-voltage versions, however, are powered by transformers and can be connected inconspicuously to a low-voltage landscape lighting circuit. They are available from specialty lighting stores and catalogs.

ROUTE THE CABLE

Run a cable from a transformer or from a nearby low-voltage circuit using a T-connector.

Route the cable up a post at the end of the rail, and secure it with cable staples. Leave enough length at the end of the cable to connect it to the rope light (**photo 1**).

SECURE THE ROPE LIGHT

Secure the rope light to the underside of the railing with U-channel. Cut the channel to length, and nail it to the bottom of the railing.

Press the rope into the channel (**photo 2**).

WIRE THE ROPE LIGHT

Connect the fixture cord to the end of the rope with the twist-on fitting.

Connect the rope wires to the branch cable with a cable connector designed for low-voltage outdoor cable (**photo 3**).

Cap the end of the rope with a plastic cap.

Run low-voltage cable from a transformer or low-voltage circuit to the end of the railing and secure with cable staples.

Fasten U channel to the bottom of the railing, then press the rope light in the channel securely.

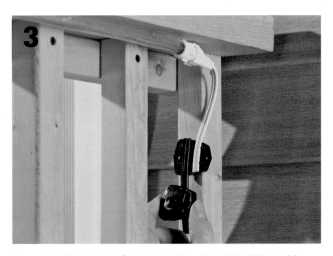

Connect the rope wires to the branch cable with a cable connector designed for outdoor cable.

Hot Tub Deck

Building a hot tub into a deck is usually done in one of two ways. If you design your deck at exactly the right height, you can create a full inset by resting the hot tub on a concrete pad and building the deck around it.

But on a low-profile deck, or a tall deck, the most practical solution is to mount the hot tub on the surface of the deck and build a secondary platform around it, creating a partial inset. As shown on the following pages, the structural design of the deck must be modified to ensure that it can support the added weight of a hot tub filled with water. Make sure your deck plans are approved by the building inspector before you begin work.

Installing a hot tub usually requires the installation of new plumbing and electrical lines. When planning the installation, make sure to consider the location of plumbing pipes, electrical cables, switches, and access panels. For convenience, arrange to have the rough-in work for these utilities done before you install the decking boards.

Whether the tub is inset into the deck or rests on top, adding a hot tub to your deck is a very popular deck improvement project.

Gallery of Hot Tub Decks

Hot tubs aren't limited to ground-level decks. However, you'll need to plan for additional framing and footings to support the tub safely, whatever the height of your deck may be. Here's another important reason why your deck plans should be reviewed by a building inspector before you build.

When planning for a hot tub, consider locating it in a space that's adjacent to your primary deck. That way, the tub won't interfere with traffic patterns or block larger spaces you may need for tables, other patio furniture, or groups of people.

If your yard doesn't offer much privacy for a hot tub, it's easy to create some by building a privacy wall onto your deck. A colored fabric wind shade could serve the same purpose. Now, you'll be able to enjoy your soaks or tanning time with a greater sense of peace.

Planning For Hot Tubs

Access hatch made from decking can hide a utility feature, such as a water faucet or air-conditioner compressor. Install cleats along the inside of the framed opening to support the hatch. Construct the hatch from decking boards mounted on a 2 × 4 frame. Finger holes drilled in the hatch make removal easier.

Plan posts and beams to support the maximum anticipated load, including the weight of the hot tub filled with water. In most cases, this means altering your deck plan to include extra beams and posts directly under the hot tub.

How to Build a Hot Tub Deck

Lay out and install the ledger, footings, posts, and support beams, according to your deck plans. Lay out joist locations on the ledger and beams, and install the joists, following local code requirements. Many building codes require joists spaced no more than 12" on center if the deck will support a hot tub. If your hot tub requires new plumbing or electrical lines, have the preliminary rough-in work done before continuing with deck construction.

2

Install the decking boards, then snap chalk lines to outline the position of the hot tub and the raised platform that will enclose the hot tub.

3

Lay out and cut 2 × 4 sole plates and top plates for the stud walls on the raised platform.

4

Mark stud locations on the top and bottom plates. Studs should be positioned every 16" (measured on center), and at the ends of each plate.

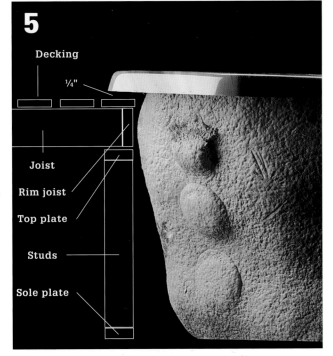

5

Decking

¼"

Joist

Rim joist

Top plate

Studs

Sole plate

Measure the height of the hot tub to determine the required height of the studs in the platform walls. Remember to include the thickness of both wall plates, the joists that will rest on the walls, and the decking material on the platform. The surface of the finished platform should be ¼" below the lip of the hot tub.

(continued)

Construct the stud walls by screwing the plates to the studs. Position the walls upright on the deck over the outline marks, and anchor them to the deck with 2½" deck screws.

At corners, join the studs together with 3" deck screws. Check the walls for plumb, and brace them in position.

Toenail a 2 × 6 rim joist along the back edge of the platform, then cut and install 2 × 6 joists across the top of the stud walls at 16" intervals, toenailing them to the top plates. The ends of the joists should be set back 1½" from the edges of the top plates to allow for the rim joist.

Blocking

Cut 2 × 6 rim joists to length, and endnail them to the joists with 16d nails. At angled wall segments, cut diagonal blocking and attach it between the rim joist and adjoining joists with deck screws.

10

Cut decking boards, and attach them to the platform joists with 2½" deck screws. If your hot tub requires cutouts for plumbing or electrical lines, do this work now.

11

Set the hot tub in place, then build 2 × 2 stud walls around the exposed sides of the tub. Measure, cut, and install siding materials on the exposed walls.

12

Build platform steps to provide access to the platform, using siding materials to box in the risers. Where required by code, install railings around the elevated platform.

Under-deck Enclosure

Second-story walkout decks can be a mixed blessing. On top, you have an open, sun-filled perch with a commanding view of the landscape. The space below the deck, however, is all too often a dark and chilly nook that is functionally unprotected from water runoff. As a result, an under-deck area often ends up as wasted space or becomes a holding area for seasonal storage items or the less desirable outdoor furniture.

But there's an easy way to reclaim all that convenient outdoor space—by installing a weatherizing ceiling system that captures runoff water from the deck above, leaving the area below dry enough to convert into a versatile outdoor room. You can even enclose the space to create a screened-in patio room.

The under-deck system featured in this project (see resources, p. 315) is designed for do-it-yourself installation. Its components are made to fit almost any standard deck and come in three sizes to accommodate different deck-joist spacing (for 12", 16", and 24" on-center spacing). Once the system is in place the under-deck area is effectively "dried in", and you can begin adding amenities like overhead lighting, ceiling fans, and speakers to complete the outdoor

room environment.

The system works by capturing water that falls through the decking above and channeling it to the outside edge of the deck. Depending on your plans, you can let the water fall from the ceiling panels along the deck's edge, or you can install a standard rain gutter and downspout to direct the water to a single exit point on the ground. Steps for adding a gutter system are given on pages 239 to 241.

Tools & Materials ▸

4-ft. level	Under-deck
Chalk line	ceiling system
Caulking gun	Waterproof
Drill	acrylic caulk
Aviation snips	1" stainless
Hacksaw	steel screws
(for optional	Rain gutter system
rain gutter)	(optional)

Made of weather-resistant vinyl, this under-deck system creates an attractive, maintenance-free ceiling that keeps the space below dry throughout the seasons.

Design Tips

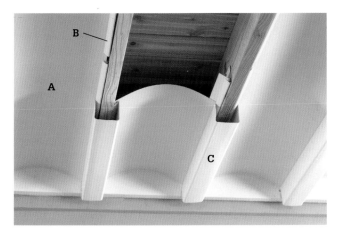

This under-deck system (see Resources, page 315) consists of four main parts: The joist rails mount to the deck joists and help secure the other components. The collector panels (A) span the joist cavity to capture water falling through the deck above. Water flows to the sides of the panels where it falls through gaps in the joist rails (B) and into the joist gutters (C) (for interior joists) and boundary gutters (for outer joists). The gutters carry the water to the outside edge of the deck.

For a finished look, paint the decking lumber that will be exposed after the system is installed. Typically, the lower portion of the ledger board (attached to the house) and the outer rim joist (at the outer edge of the deck) remain exposed.

Consider surrounding architectural elements when you select a system for sealing off the area below your deck. Here, the under-deck system is integrated with the deck and deck stairs both visually and functionally.

How to Install an Under-deck System

1

Check the undersides of several deck joists to make sure the structure is level. This is important for establishing the proper slope for effective water flow.

2

If your deck is not level, you must compensate for this when setting the ceiling slope. To determine the amount of correction that's needed, hold one end of the level against a joist and tilt the level until it reads perfectly level. Measure the distance from the joist to the free end of the level. Then, divide this measurement by the length of the level. For example, if the distance is ¼" and the level is 4 ft. long, the deck is out of level by ¹⁄₁₆" per foot.

3

To establish the slope for the ceiling system, mark the ends of the joists closest to the house: Measure up from the bottom 1" for every 10 ft. of joist length (or approximately ⅛" per ft.) and make a mark. Mark both sides of each intermediate joist and the inside faces of the outer joists.

4

Create each slope reference line using a chalk line: Hold one end of the chalk line at the mark made in Step 3, and hold the other end at the bottom edge of the joist where it meets the rim joist at the outside edge of the deck. Snap a reference line on all of the joists.

Install vinyl flashing along the ledger board in the joist cavities. Attach the flashing with 1" stainless steel screws. Caulk along the top edges of the flashing where it meets the ledger and both joists, using quality, waterproof acrylic caulk. Also caulk the underside of the flashing for an extra layer of protection.

Begin installing the joist rails, starting 1" away from the ledger. Position each rail with its bottom edge on the chalk line, and fasten it to the joist at both ends with 1" stainless steel screws, then add one or two screws in between. Avoid over-driving the screws and deforming the rail; leaving a little room for movement is best.

Install the remaining rails on each joist face, leaving a 1½" (minimum) to 2" (maximum) gap between rails. Install rails along both sides of each interior joist and along the insides of each outside joist. Trim the final rail in each row as needed, using aviation snips.

Measure the full length of each joist cavity, and cut a collector panel ¼" shorter than the cavity. This allows room for expansion of the panels. For narrower joist cavities, trim the panel to width following the manufacturer's sizing recommendations.

(continued)

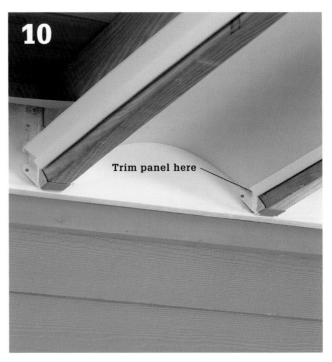

Scribe and trim collector panels for a tight fit against the ledger board. Hold a carpenter's pencil flat against the ledger, and move the pencil along the board to transfer its contours to the panel. Trim the panel along the scribed line.

Trim the corners of collector panels as needed to accommodate joist hangers and other hardware. This may be necessary only at the house side of the joist cavity; at the outer end, the ¼" expansion gap should clear any hardware.

Install the collector panels, starting at the house. With the textured side of the panel facing down, insert one side edge into the joist rails, and then push up gently on the opposite side until it fits into the opposing rails. When fully installed, the panels should be tight against the ledger and have a ¼" gap at the rim joist.

Prepare each joist gutter by cutting it ¼" shorter than the joist it will attach to. If the joists rest on a structural beam, see Variation, on page 238. On the house end of each gutter, trim the corners of the flanges at 45°. This helps the gutter fit tightly to the ledger.

13

Cut four or five ⅛" tabs into the bottom surface at the outside ends of the gutters. This helps promote the drainage of water over the edge of the gutter.

14

Caulk here

Attach self-adhesive foam weatherstrip (available from the manufacturer) at the home-end of each joist gutter. Run a bead of caulk along the foam strip to water-seal it to the gutter. The weatherstrip serves as a water dam.

15

Install each joist gutter by spreading its sides open slightly while pushing the gutter up onto the joist rails until it snaps into place. The gutter should fit snugly against the collector panels. The gutter's home-end should be tight against the ledger, with the ¼" expansion gap at the rim joist.

16

Prepare the boundary gutters following the same steps used for the joist gutters. Install each boundary gutter by slipping its long, outside flange behind the joist rails and pushing up until the gutter snaps into place. Install the boundary gutters working from the house side to the outer edge of the deck.

(continued)

17

Run a bead of color-matched caulk along the joint where the collector panels meet the ledger board. This is for decorative purposes only and is not required to prevent water intrusion.

18

If collector panels are misshapen because the joist spacing is too tight, free the panel within the problem area, then trim about ⅛" from the side edge of the panel. Reset the panel in the rails. If necessary, trim the panel edge again in slight increments until the panel fits properly.

Working Around Beams ▶

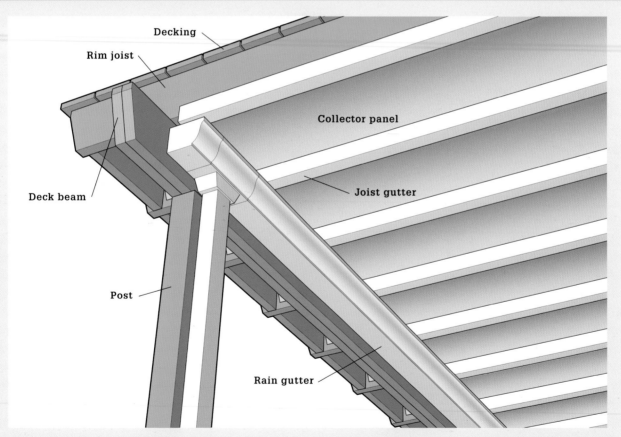

Decking

Rim joist

Collector panel

Deck beam

Joist gutter

Post

Rain gutter

For decks that have joists resting on top of a structural beam, stop the joist gutters and boundary gutters 1½" short of the beam. Install a standard rain gutter along the house-side of the beam to catch the water as it exits the system gutters (see pages 239 to 241). (On the opposite side of the beam, begin new runs of joist gutters that are tight against the beam and stop ¼" short of the rim joist. The joist rails and collector panels should clear the beam and can be installed as usual.) Or, you can simply leave the overhang area alone if you do not need water runoff protection below it.

Runoff Gutters

A basic gutter system for a square or rectangular deck includes a straight run of gutter channel with a downspout at one end. Prefabricated vinyl or aluminum gutter parts are ideal for this application. Gutter channels are commonly available in 10-ft. and 20-ft. lengths, so you might be able to use a single channel without seams. Otherwise, you can join sections of channel with special connectors. Shop around for the best type of hanger for your situation. If there's limited backing to support the back side of the channel or to fasten into, you may have to use strap-type hangers that can be secured to framing above the gutter.

How to Install an Under-deck Runoff Gutter

1

Snap a chalk line onto the beam or other supporting surface to establish the slope of the main gutter run. The line will correspond to the top edge of the gutter channel. The ideal slope is 1/16" per foot. For example, with a 16-ft.-long gutter, the beginning is 1" higher than the end. The downspout should be located just inside the low end of the gutter channel. Mark the beam at both ends to create the desired slope, then snap a chalk line between the marks. The high end of the gutter should be just below the boundary gutter in the ceiling system.

(continued)

2

Install a downspout outlet near the end of the gutter run so the top of the gutter is flush with the slope line. If you plan to enclose the area under the deck, choose an inconspicuous location for the downspout, away from traffic areas.

3

Install hanger clips (depending on the type of hangers or support clips you use, it is often best to install them before installing the gutter channel). Attach a hanger every 24" so the top of the gutter will hang flush with slope line.

Gutter Options ▶

Gutters come in several material types, including PVC, enameled steel, and copper. In most cases you should try and match the surrounding trim materials, but using a more decorative material for contrast can be effective.

4

Cut sections of gutter channel to size, using a hacksaw. Attach an end cap to the beginning of the main run, then fit the channel into the downspout outlet (allowing for expansion, if necessary) and secure the gutter in place.

5

Join sections of channel together, if necessary, for long runs, using connectors. Install a short section of channel with an end cap on the opposite side of the downspout outlet. Paint the area where downspout will be installed if it is unpainted.

6

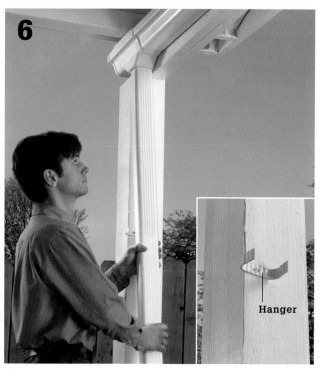

Hanger

Cut the downspout piping to length and fasten an elbow fitting to its bottom end. Attach the downspout to the downspout outlet, then secure the downspout to a post or other vertical support, using hangers (inset).

7

Cut a drain pipe to run from the downspout elbow to a convenient drainage point. Position the pipe so it directs water away from the house and any traffic areas. Attach the pipe to the downspout elbow. Add a splash block, if desired.

Rerouting Downspouts ▸

You may have to get a little creative when routing the downspout drain in an enclosed porch or patio. Shown here, two elbows allow for a 90° turn of the drainpipe.

Ground Level Walkout Deck

Here's a deck that's classic in its simplicity. Moderately sized and easy to build, this rectangular deck won't cost you an arm and a leg—in either time or money. The framing and decking plans are quite straightforward, and you can likely build the entire deck in just two or three weekends, even with

limited carpentry and building experience. Within just a few weeks time, you can transform your yard into a congenial gathering place for cooking, entertaining and just plain relaxing; a place where you, your family, and your friends can enjoy the fresh air in convenience and comfort.

Extend your living space and increase your home's value.

Cutaway View

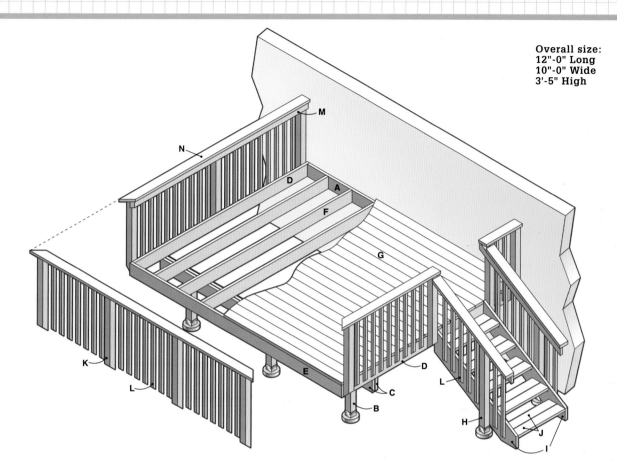

Overall size:
12"-0" Long
10"-0" Wide
3'-5" High

Supplies

10"-diameter footing forms (3)
8"-diameter footing forms (2)
J-bolts (5)
6 × 6" metal post anchors (3)
4 × 4" metal post anchors (2)
6 × 6" metal post-beam caps (3)
2 × 8" joist hangers (16)
1½ × 6" angle brackets (6)
1½ × 10" angle brackets (10)
3" galvanized deck screws
16d galvanized nails
2½" galvanized deck screws
2½" galvanized screws
⅜ × 4" lag screws and washers (20)
⅜ × 5" lag screws and washers (22)
¼ × 1¼" lag screws and washers (80)
Flashing (12 ft.)
Exterior silicone caulk (3 tubes)
Concrete as needed

Lumber List

Qty.	Size	Material	Part
4	2 × 8" × 12'	Trtd. lumber	Ledger (A), Beam bds (C), Rim joist (E)
1	6 × 6" × 8'	Trtd. lumber	Deck posts (B)
10	2 × 8" × 10'	Trtd. lumber	End joists (D), Joists (F)
25	2 × 6" × 12'	Cedar	Decking (G), Rail cap (N)
7	4 × 4" × 8'	Cedar	Stair posts (H), Rail post (K)
2	2 × 12" × 8'	Cedar	Stringers (I)
5	2 × 6" × 6'	Cedar	Treads (J)
32	2 × 2" × 8'	Cedar	Balusters (L)
2	2 × 4" × 12'	Cedar	Top rail (M)
2	2 × 4" × 10'	Cedar	Top rail (M)

Framing Plan

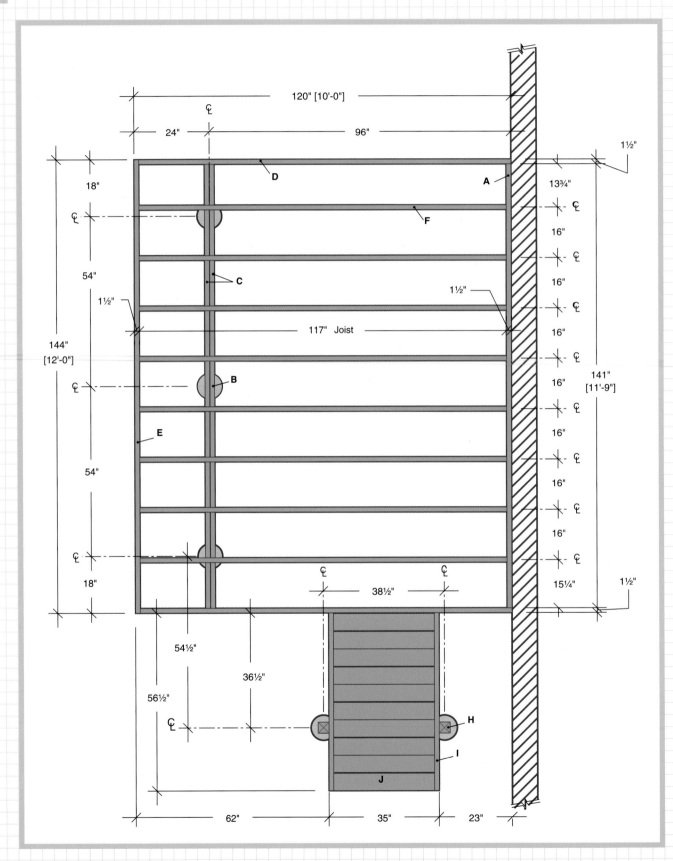

Elevation

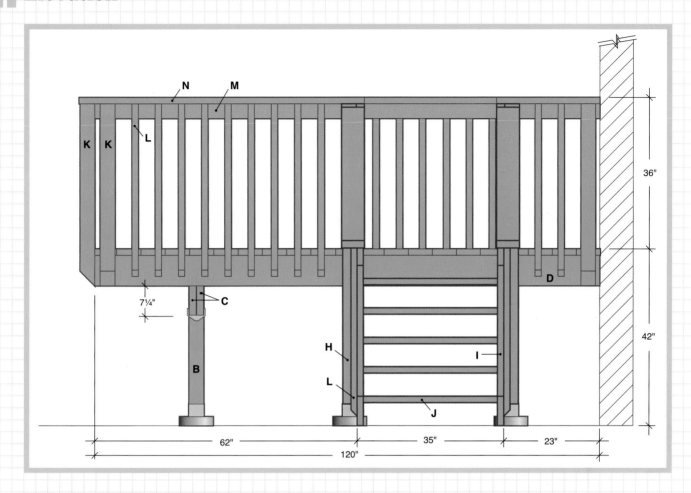

Stairway Detail

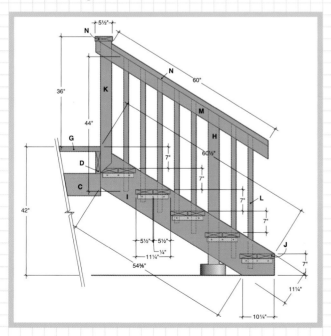

Railing Detail

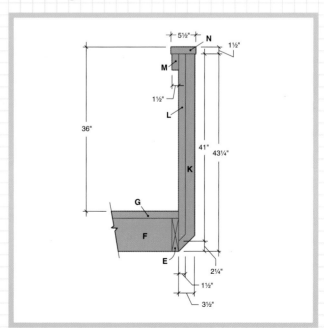

How to Build a Ground-level Walkout Deck

ATTACH THE LEDGER

Draw a level outline on the siding to show where the ledger and the end joists will fit against the house. Install the ledger so that the surface of the decking boards will be 1" below the indoor floor level. This height difference prevents rainwater or melted snow from seeping into the house.

Cut out the siding along the outline with a circular saw. To prevent the blade from cutting the sheathing that lies underneath the siding, set the blade depth to the same thickness as the siding. Finish the cutout with a chisel, holding the beveled side in to ensure a straight cut.

Cut galvanized flashing to the length of the cutout, using metal snips. Slide the flashing up under the siding at the top of the cutout.

Measure and cut the ledger (A) from pressure-treated lumber. Center the ledger end to end in the cutout, with space at each end for the end joist.

Brace the ledger in position under the flashing. Tack the ledger into place with galvanized deck screws.

Drill pairs of ¼" pilot holes at 16" intervals through the ledger and into the house header joist. Counterbore each pilot hole ½", using a 1" spade bit. Attach the ledger to the wall with ⅜ × 4" lag screws and washers, using a ratchet wrench.

Apply a thick bead of silicone caulk between siding and flashing. Also seal the lag screw heads and the cracks at the ends of the ledger.

POUR THE FOOTINGS

Referring to the measurements shown in the Framing Plan, page 244, mark the centerlines of the two outer footings on the ledger and drive nails at these locations.

Set up temporary batterboards and stretch a mason's string out from the ledger at each location. Make sure the strings are perpendicular to the ledger, and measure along the strings to find the centerpoints of the posts.

Set up additional batterboards and stretch another string parallel to the ledger across the post centerpoints.

Check the mason's strings for square, by measuring diagonally from corner to corner and adjusting the strings so that the measurements are equal.

Measure along the cross string and mark the center post location with a piece of tape.

Use a plumb bob to transfer the footing centerpoints to the ground, and drive a stake to mark each point.

Remove the mason's strings and dig the post footings, using a clamshell digger or power auger. Pour 2" to 3" of loose gravel into each hole for drainage. *Note: When measuring the footing size and depth, make sure you comply with your local building code, which may require flaring the base.*

Cut the footing forms to length, using a reciprocating saw or handsaw, and insert them into the footing holes, leaving 2" above ground level. Pack soil around the forms for support, and fill the forms with concrete, tamping with a long stick or rod to eliminate any air pockets.

Screed the tops flush with a straight 2 × 4. Insert a J-bolt into each footing, set so ¾" to 1" of thread is exposed. Retie the mason's strings and position the J-bolts at the exact center of the posts, using a plumb bob as a guide. Clean the bolt threads before concrete sets.

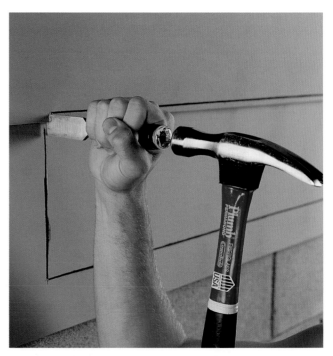

After outlining the position of the ledger and cutting the siding with a circular saw, use a chisel to finish the corners of the cutout.

After the posts have been set in place and braced plumb, use a straight 2 × 4 and a level to mark the top of the beam on each post.

SET THE POSTS

Lay a long, straight 2 × 4 flat across the footings, parallel to the ledger. With one edge tight against the J-bolts, draw a reference line across each footing.

Place a metal post anchor on each footing, centering it over the J-bolt and squaring it with the reference line. Attach the post anchors by threading a nut over each bolt and tightening with a ratchet wrench.

Cut the posts to length, adding approximately 6" for final trimming. Place the posts in the anchors and tack into place with one nail.

With a level as a guide, use braces and stakes to plumb the posts. Finish nailing the posts to the anchors.

Determine the height of the beam by extending a straight 2 × 4 from the bottom edge of the ledger across the face of a post. Level the 2 × 4, and draw a line on the post.

From that line, measure 7¼" down the post and mark the bottom of the beam. Using a level, transfer this line to the remaining posts.

Use a combination square to extend the level line completely around each post. Cut the posts to this finished height, using a reciprocating saw or hand saw.

INSTALL THE BEAM

Cut the beam boards (C) several inches longer than necessary, to allow for final trimming.

Join the beam boards together with 2½" galvanized deck screws. Mark the post locations on the top edges and sides, using a combination square as a guide.

Attach the post-beam caps to the tops of the posts. Position the caps on the post tops, and attach using 10d joist hanger nails.

Lift the beam into the post-beam caps, with the crown up. Align the post reference lines on the beam with the post-beam caps. *Note: You should have at least two helpers when installing boards of this size and length, at this height.*

Fasten the post-beam caps to the beam on both sides using 10d joist hanger nails.

INSTALL THE FRAME

Measure and cut the end joists to length using a circular saw.

Attach end joists to the ends of the ledger with 10d common nails.

Measure and cut the rim joist (E) to length with a circular saw. Fasten to end joists with 16d galvanized nails.

Square up the frame by measuring corner to corner and adjusting until measurements are equal. Toenail the end joists in place on top of the beam, and trim the beam to length.

Reinforce each inside corner of the frame with an angle bracket fastened with 10d joist hanger nails.

Install joists in hangers with crown side up.

(continued)

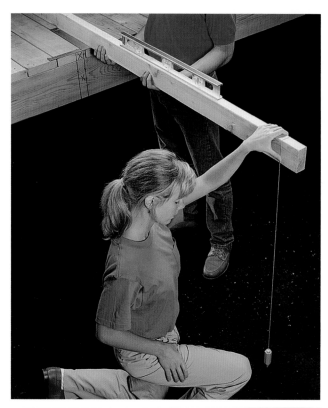

To locate the stairway footings, refer to the measurements in the Framing Plan, and extend a straight 2 × 4 perpendicularly from the deck. Use a plumb bob to transfer centerpoints to the ground.

INSTALL THE JOISTS

Mark the outlines of the inner joists (F) on the ledger, beam, and rim joist (see Framing Plan, page 244), using a tape measure and a combination square.

Attach joist hangers to the ledger and rim joist with 10d joist hanger nails, using a scrap 2 × 8 as a spacer to achieve the correct spread for each hanger.

Measure, mark and cut lumber for inner joists, using a circular saw. Place the joists in the hangers with crown side up, and attach at both ends with 10d joist hanger nails. Be sure to use all the holes in the hangers.

Align the joists with the marks on top of the beam, and toenail in place.

LAY THE DECKING

Cut the first decking board (G) to length, position it against the house, and attach by driving a pair of 2½" galvanized deck screws into each joist.

Position the remaining decking boards with the ends overhanging the end joists. Leave a ⅛" gap between boards to provide for drainage, and attach the boards to each joist with a pair of deck screws.

Every few rows of decking, measure from the edge of the decking to the outside edge of the deck. If the measurement can be divided evenly by 5⅝, the last board will fit flush with the outside edge of the deck as intended. If the measurement shows that the last board will not fit flush, adjust the spacing as you install the remaining rows of boards.

If your decking overhangs the end joists, snap a chalk line to mark the outside edge of the deck and cut flush with a circular saw. If needed, finish the cut with a jigsaw or handsaw where a circular saw can't reach.

BUILD THE STAIRWAY

Refer to the Framing Plan, page 244, for the position of the stairway footings.

Locate the footings by extending a 2 × 4 from the deck, dropping a plumb bob, and marking the centerpoints with stakes.

Dig post holes with a clamshell digger or an auger, and pour the stairway footings using the same method as for the deck footings.

Attach metal post anchors to the footings, and install posts (H), leaving them long for final trimming.

Cut the stair stringers (I) to length and use a framing square to mark the rise and run for each step (see Stairway Detail, page 245). Draw the tread outline on each run. Cut the angles at the end of the stringers with a circular saw. (For more information on building stairways, see pages 120 to 137.)

After attaching the stringers to the deck, fasten them to the posts. Drill and counterbore two pilot holes through the stringers into the posts, and attach with lag screws.

Position a 1½ × 10" angle bracket flush with the bottom of each tread line. Attach the brackets with 1¼" lag screws.

Fasten angle brackets to the upper ends of the stringers, using 1¼" lag screws; keep the brackets flush with cut ends on stringers. Position the top ends of the stringers on the side of the deck, making sure the top point of the stringer and the surface of the deck are flush.

Attach the stringers by driving 10d joist hanger nails through the angle brackets into the end joist, and by drilling ¼" pilot holes from inside the rim joist into the stringers and fastening with ⅜ × 4" lag screws.

To connect the stringers to the stair posts, drill two ¼" pilot holes and counterbore the pilot holes ½" deep with a 1" spade bit. Use a ratchet wrench to fasten the stringers to the posts with 4" lag screws and washers.

Measure the length of the stair treads (J) and cut two 2 × 6 boards for each tread. For each tread, position the front board on the angle bracket so the front edge is flush with the tread outline on the stringers. Attach the tread to the brackets with ¼ × 1¼" lag screws.

Place the rear 2 × 6 on each tread bracket, keeping a ⅛" space between the boards. Attach with 1¼" lag screws.

Attach the treads for the lowest step by driving deck screws through the stringers.

INSTALL THE RAILING

Cut posts (K) and balusters (L) to length (see Railing Detail, page 245) with a power miter saw or circular saw. Cut the top ends square, and the bottom ends at a 45° angle.

Mark and drill two ¼" pilot holes at the bottom end of each post. Holes should be spaced 4" apart and counterbored ½", with a 1" spade bit.

Drill two ⅛" pilot holes, 4" apart, near the bottom of each baluster. At the top of each baluster, drill a pair of ⅛" pilot holes spaced 1½" apart.

Using a combination square, mark the locations of the posts on the outside of the deck. *Note: Position corner posts so there is no more than 4" clearance between them.*

Clamp each post in place. Keep the beveled end flush with the bottom of the deck, and make sure the post is plumb. Use an awl to mark pilot hole locations on the side of the deck. Remove posts and drill ¼" pilot holes at marks. Attach the railing posts to the side of the deck with ⅜ × 5" lag screws and washers.

Position the rail cap over the posts and balusters. Make sure mitered corners are tight, and attach with deck screws.

Cut top rails (M) to length, with 45° miters on the ends that meet at the corners. Attach to posts with 2½" deck screws, keeping the top edge of the rail flush with the top of the posts. Join rails by cutting 45° bevels at ends.

Temporarily attach stairway top rails with 3" galvanized screws. Mark the outline of the deck railing post and top rail on the back side of the stairway top rail. Mark the position of the top rail on the stairway post. Use a level to mark a plumb cutoff line at the lower end of the rail. Remove the rail.

Cut the stairway post to finished height along the diagonal mark, and cut the stairway rail along outlines. Reposition the stairway rail and attach with deck screws.

Attach the balusters between the railing posts at equal intervals of 4" or less. Use deck screws, and keep the top ends of balusters flush with the top rail. On the stairway, position the balusters against the stringer and top rail, and check for plumb. Draw a diagonal cut line at top of baluster and trim to final height with a power miter saw.

Confirm measurements, and cut rail cap sections (N) to length. Position sections so that the inside edge overhangs the inside edge of the rail by ¼". Attach cap to rail with deck screws. At corners, miter the ends 45° and attach caps to posts.

Cut the cap for stairway rail to length. Mark angle of deck railing post on side of cap and bevel-cut the ends of the cap. Attach cap to top rail and post with deck screws. *Note: Local building codes may require a grippable handrail. Check with your building inspector.*

Second-story Walkout Deck

This simple rectangular deck provides a secure, convenient outdoor living space. The absence of a stairway prevents children from wandering away or unexpected visitors from wandering in. It also makes the deck easier to build.

Imagine how handy it will be to have this additional living area only a step away from your dining room or living room, with no more need to walk downstairs for outdoor entertaining, dining or relaxing.

And if you'd like to add a stairway, just refer to the chapter on stair-building (see page 119).

Simplicity, security, and convenience are the hallmarks of this elevated deck.

Cutaway View

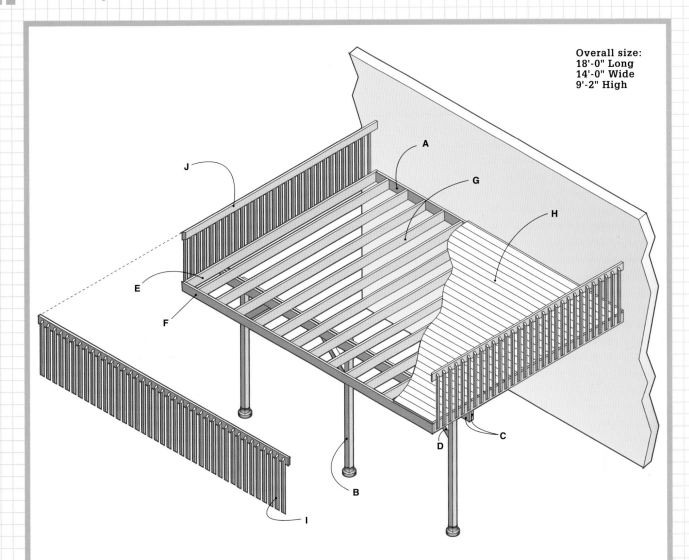

Overall size:
18'-0" Long
14'-0" Wide
9'-2" High

Supplies

12"-diameter footing forms (3)
J-bolts (3)
6 × 6" metal post anchors (3)
2 × 10" joist hangers (26)
Galvanized deck screws (3", 2½" and 1¼")
Joist hanger nails
⅜ × 4" lag screws and washers (28)
¼ × 5" lag screws and washers (16)
⁵⁄₁₆ × 7" carriage bolts, washers, and nuts (6)
16d galvanized nails
Metal flashing (18 ft.)
Silicone caulk (3 tubes)
Concrete as required

Lumber List

Qty.	Size	Material	Part
2	2 × 12" × 20'	Trtd. lumber	Beam boards (C)
2	2 × 10" × 18'	Trtd. lumber	Ledger (A), Rim joist (F)
15	2 × 10" × 14'	Trtd. lumber	Joists (G), End joists (E)
3	6 × 6" × 10'	Trtd. lumber	Deck posts (B)
2	4 × 4" × 8'	Trtd. lumber	Braces (D)
32	2 × 6" × 18'	Cedar	Decking (H), Top rail (J)
2	2 × 6" × 16'	Cedar	Top rail (J)
50	2 × 2" × 8'	Cedar	Balusters (I)

Framing Plan

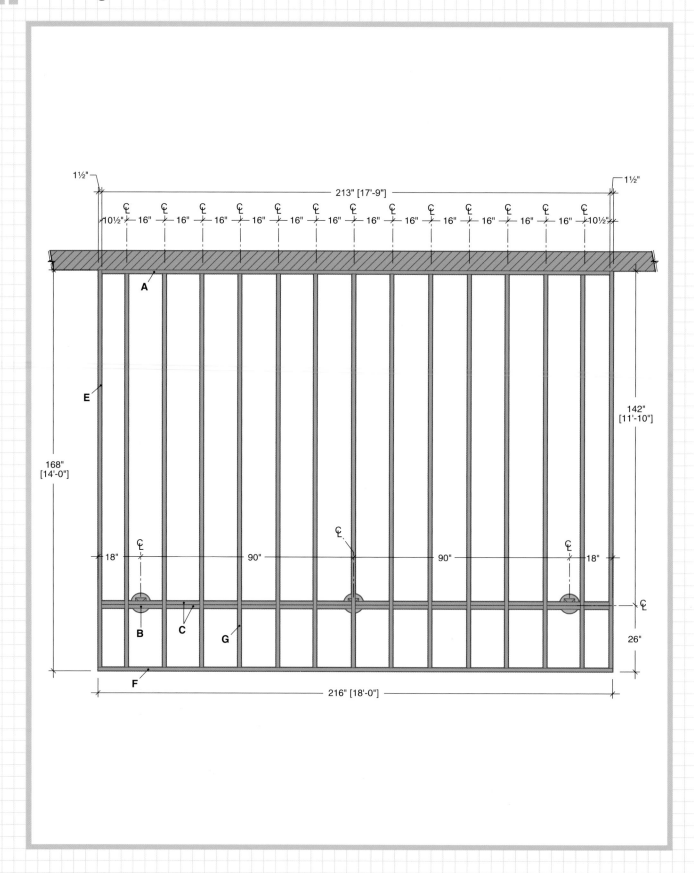

Elevation

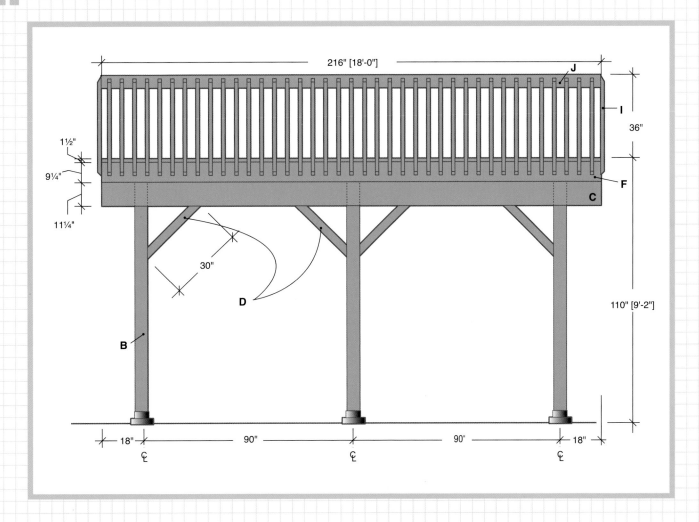

Railing Detail

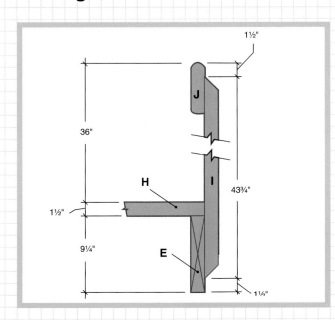

Face Board Detail

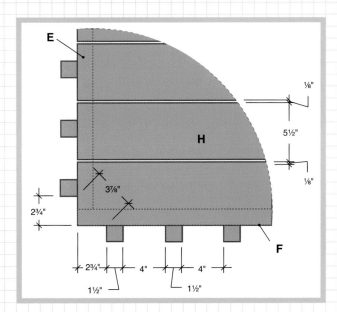

How to Build a Second-story Walkout Deck

ATTACH THE LEDGER

Draw a level outline on the siding to show where the ledger and the end joists will fit against the house. Install the ledger so that the surface of the decking boards will be 1" below the indoor floor level. This height difference prevents rainwater or melted snow from seeping into the house.

Cut out the siding along the outline with a circular saw. To avoid cutting the sheathing that lies underneath the siding, set the blade depth to the same thickness as the siding. Finish the cutout with a chisel, holding the beveled side in to ensure a straight cut.

Cut galvanized flashing to the length of the cutout, using metal snips. Slide the flashing up under the siding at the top of the cutout.

Measure and cut the ledger (A) from pressure-treated lumber. Center the ledger end to end in the cutout, with space at each end for the end joist.

Brace the ledger into position under the flashing. Tack the ledger into place with galvanized nails.

Drill pairs of ¼" pilot holes at 16" intervals through the ledger and into the house header joist. Counterbore each pilot hole ½", using a 1" spade bit. Attach the ledger with 4" lag screws and washers, using a ratchet wrench.

Apply silicone caulk between the siding and flashing. Also seal the lag screw heads and the cracks at the ends of the ledger.

POUR THE FOOTINGS

To establish a reference point for locating the footings, drop a plumb bob from the ends of the ledger down to the ground.

Position a straight 14 ft.-long 2 × 4 perpendicular to the house at the point where the plumb bob meets the ground. *Note: If you are building on a steep slope or uneven ground, the mason's string method of locating footing positions will work better (see pages 46 to 51).*

Check for square, using the 3-4-5 triangle method. From the 2 × 4, measure 3 ft. along the wall and make a mark. Next, measure 4 ft. out from the house and make a mark on the 2 × 4. The diagonal line between the marks will measure 5 ft. when the board is accurately square to the house. Adjust the board as needed, using stakes to hold it in place.

Extend another reference board from the house at the other end of the ledger, following the same procedure.

Measure out along both boards, and mark the centerline of the footings (see Framing Plan, page 252).

Lay a straight 2 × 4 between the centerline marks, and drive stakes to mark the footing locations.

Remove the boards and dig the post footings, using a clamshell digger or power auger. Pour 2" to 3" of loose gravel into each hole for drainage. *Note: When measuring the footing size and depth, make sure you comply with local building codes, which may require flaring the base to 18".*

Use a template made from 2 × 4s to locate the post footings on the ground, then mark the footings with stakes.

Plumb each post with a level, then use braces and stakes to hold in place until the beam and joists are installed.

Cut the footing forms to length, using a reciprocating saw or handsaw, and insert them into the footing holes, leaving 2" above ground level. Pack soil around the forms for support, and fill the forms with concrete, tamping with a long stick or rod to eliminate any air gaps.

Screed the tops flush with a straight 2 × 4. Insert a J-bolt into the center of each footing and set with ¾" to 1" of thread exposed. Clean the bolt threads before the concrete sets.

SET THE POSTS

Lay a long, straight 2 × 4 flat across the footings, parallel to the house. With one edge tight against the J-bolts, draw a reference line across the top of each footing to help orient the post anchors.

Place a metal post anchor on each footing, centering it over the J-bolt and squaring it with the reference line. Attach the post anchors by threading a nut over each bolt and tightening with a ratchet wrench.

The tops of the posts (B) will eventually be level with the bottom edge of the ledger, but initially cut the posts several inches longer to allow for final trimming. Position the posts in the anchors and tack into place with one nail each.

With a level as a guide, use braces and stakes to ensure that the posts are plumb.

Determine the height of the beam by using a chalk line and a line level. Extend the chalk line out from the bottom edge of the ledger, make sure that the line is level, and snap a mark across the face of a post. Use the line and level to transfer the mark to the remaining posts.

NOTCH THE POSTS

Remove the posts from the post anchors and cut to the finished height.

Measure and mark a 3" × 11¼" notch at the top of each post, on the outside face. Use a framing square to trace lines on all sides. Rough-cut the notches with a circular saw, then finish with a reciprocating saw or handsaw.

Reattach the posts to the post anchors, with the notch-side facing away from the deck.

INSTALL THE BEAM

Cut the beam boards (C) to length, adding several inches to each end for final trimming after the deck frame is squared up.

Join the beam boards together with 2½" galvanized deck screws. Mark the post locations on the top edges and sides, using a combination square as a guide.

Lift the beam, one end at a time, into the notches with the crown up. Align and clamp the beam to the posts. *Note: Installing boards of this size and length, at this height, requires caution. You should have at least two helpers.*

Counterbore two ½"-deep holes using a 1" spade bit, then drill 5⁄16" pilot holes through the beam and post.

Thread a carriage bolt into each pilot hole. Add a washer and nut to the counterbore-side of each bolt and tighten with a ratchet wrench. Seal both ends of the bolts with silicone caulk.

Cut the tops of the posts flush with the top edge of the beam, using a reciprocating saw or handsaw.

(continued)

Inside Corner Deck

With the help of a diamond decking pattern, this inside corner deck provides a focal point for recreational activities and social gatherings. At the same time, the corner location can offer intimacy, privacy, shade, and a shield from the wind.

The design calls for double joists and blocking for extra strength and stability where decking boards butt together. Joists are spaced 12" on center to support diagonal decking.

It takes a little more time to cut the decking boards and match the miter cuts, but the results are spectacular and well worth the effort.

A distinctive diamond decking pattern gives this deck visual appeal.

Cutaway View

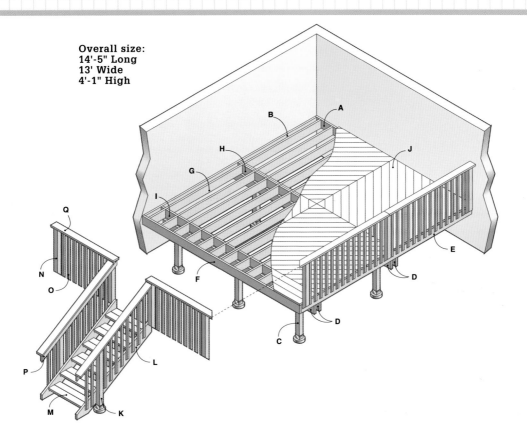

Overall size:
14'-5" Long
13' Wide
4'-1" High

Supplies

10"-diameter footing forms (6)
8"-diameter footing forms (2)
J-bolts (8)
6 × 6" metal post anchors (6)
4 × 4" metal post anchors (2)
2 × 8" single joist hangers (50)
2 × 8" double joist hangers (30)
1½ × 10" angle brackets (12)
3" galvanized deck screws
2½" galvanized deck screws
16d galvanized nails
Joist hanger nails
⅜ × 4" lag screws and washers (78)
¼ × 1¼" lag screws (96)
½ × 7" carriage bolts, washers, and nuts (12)
Exterior silicone caulk (6 tubes)
Concrete as needed

Lumber List

Qty.	Size	Material	Part
6	2 × 8" × 14'	Trtd. lumber	Short ledger (A), Long ledger (B), Beam boards (D)
14	2 × 8" × 16'	Trtd. lumber	Joists (G), Single blocking (I)
3	2 × 8" × 8'	Trtd. lumber	Double blocking (H)
3	6 × 6" × 8'	Trtd. lumber	Deck posts (C)
1	2 × 8" × 16'	Cedar	End joist (E)
1	2 × 8" × 14'	Cedar	Rim joist (F)
42	2 × 6" × 8'	Cedar	Decking (J), Railing caps (Q)
16	2 × 6" × 14'	Cedar	Decking (J)
1	4 × 4" × 10'	Cedar	Stair posts (K)
6	2 × 6" × 8'	Cedar	Treads (M)
4	4 × 4" × 8'	Cedar	Railing posts (N)
2	2 × 10" × 8'	Cedar	Stringers (L)
33	2 × 2" × 8'	Cedar	Balusters (O)
6	2 × 4" × 8'	Cedar	Top rails (P)

Framing Plan

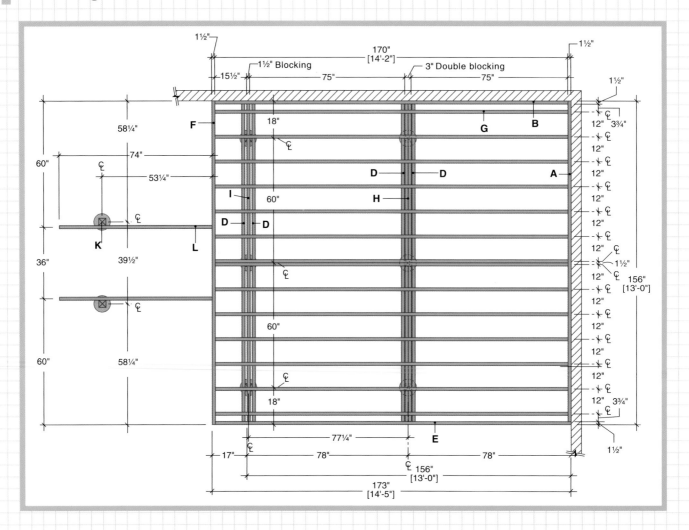

Elevation

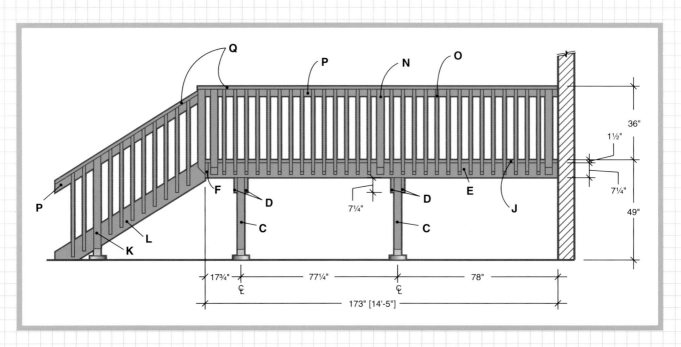

Railing Detail

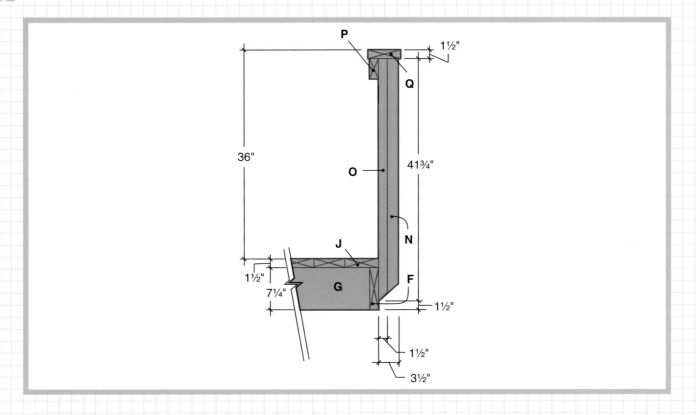

Stairway Detail

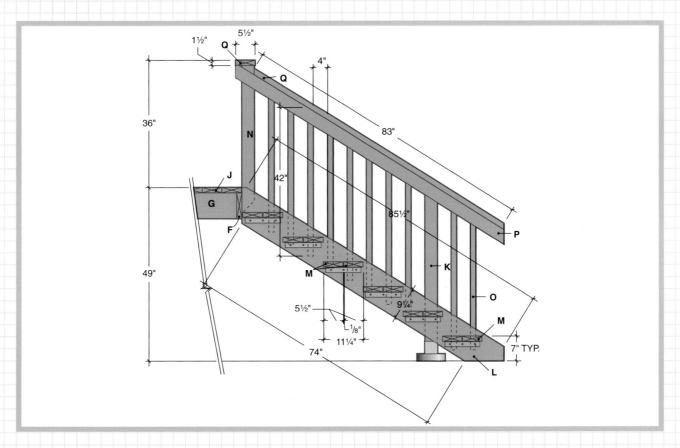

How to Build an Inside Corner Deck

ATTACH THE LEDGERS

The inside angle of the house should form a right angle. If there is a slight deviation, use shims behind the ledger to create a 90° angle in the corner.

To show where the ledgers will be attached to the house, draw outlines on the wall, using a level as a guide. To locate the top of the ledger outline, measure down from the indoor floor surface 1" plus the thickness of the decking boards. This height difference prevents rain and melting snow from seeping into the house.

Measure and cut the ledgers to length. They will be shorter than the outline on the wall to allow for the width of the rim joist and end joist.

Drill pairs of ¼" pilot holes through the ledgers at 16" intervals. Counterbore the pilot holes ½" with a 1" spade bit.

Brace the short ledger (A) in place, and insert a nail or an awl through the pilot holes to mark the hole locations on the wall.

Repeat the process to mark the hole locations for the long ledger (B).

Remove the ledgers and drill pilot holes into the stucco with a ⅜" masonry bit. Then, use a ¼" bit to extend each pilot hole through the sheathing and into the header joist.

Position and brace the ledgers against the walls. Use a ratchet wrench to attach the ledgers to the walls with ⅜ × 4" lag screws and washers. Seal the screw heads and all cracks between the wall and ledger with silicone caulk.

POUR THE DECK FOOTINGS

To locate the footings, stretch mason's strings between the ledgers and 2 × 4 supports, known as batterboards.

Referring to the measurements shown in the Framing Plan, page 260, mark the centerlines of the footings on the ledgers, and drive a nail into the ledger at each location.

Set up temporary batterboards and stretch a mason's string out from the ledger at each location. Make sure the strings are perpendicular to the ledger.

Check the mason's strings for square, using the 3-4-5 triangle method. From the point where each string meets the ledger, measure 3' along the ledger and make a mark. Next, measure 4' out along the string and mark with tape. The distance between the points on the ledger and the string should be 5'. If it's not, adjust the string position on the batterboard accordingly.

Drop a plumb bob to transfer the footing centerpoints to the ground, and drive a stake to mark each point. Remove the strings.

Position the beam against the posts, and attach it temporarily with deck screws. *Note: This method of joinery is no longer allowed in some regions. Consult your building department.*

Dig the post footings, using a clamshell digger or power auger. Pour 2" to 3" of loose gravel into each hole for drainage. *Note: Make sure the footing size and depth comply with your local building code, which may require flaring the base.*

Cut the footing forms to length, using a reciprocating saw or handsaw, and insert them into the footing holes so that they extend 2" above grade. Pack soil around the forms for support, and fill the forms with concrete, tamping with a long stick or rod to eliminate any air pockets.

Screed the tops of the footings flush, using a 2 × 4. Insert a J-bolt into the wet concrete of each footing, and set it, with ¾" to 1" of thread exposed. Retie the mason's strings and position each J-bolt at the exact center of the post location, using the plumb bob as a guide. Clean the bolt threads before the concrete sets.

SET THE POSTS

Lay a long, straight 2 × 4 flat across each row of footings, parallel to the short ledger. With one edge tight against the J-bolts, draw a reference line across the top of each footing.

Center a metal post anchor over the J-bolt on each footing, and square it with the reference line. Attach the post anchors by threading a nut over each bolt and tightening with a ratchet wrench.

Working from a plywood platform, install double blocking to support the ends of the deck boards. Attach the blocking by alternating end nailing with using joist hangers.

Cut the posts, leaving an extra 6" for final trimming. Place each post in an anchor and tack it in place with one nail.

With a level as a guide, use braces and stakes to ensure that each post is plumb. Finish nailing the posts to the anchors.

Determine the height of the inside beam by extending a straight 2 × 4 from the bottom edge of the long ledger across the row of posts. Level the 2 × 4, and draw a line on the posts. Use the same method to determine the height of the outer beam.

INSTALL THE BEAMS

Cut the beam boards (D), leaving an extra few inches for final trimming.

Position one beam board, crown up, against the row of posts. Tack the board in place with deck screws.

Attach the remaining beam boards to the posts in the same way.

Drill two ½" holes through the boards and posts at each joint, and counterbore the pilot holes ½" with a 1" spade bit. Secure the beam boards to the posts with carriage bolts, using a ratchet wrench.

Cut the tops of the posts flush with the tops of the beams, using a reciprocating saw or handsaw.

INSTALL THE JOISTS

A double joist at the center of the deck provides extra support for the ends of the decking boards.

Measure, mark, and cut the end joist (E) and the rim joist (F), using a circular saw.

Attach the end joist to the short ledger and the rim joist to the long ledger, using 16d galvanized nails.

Nail the rim joist to the end joist.

Toenail the end joist to the tops of the beams, and cut the ends of the beams flush with the end joist.

Measure, mark, and install the double center joist at the precise center of the deck with double joist hangers.

Measure both ways from the double joist, and mark the centerpoints of the remaining joists at 12" intervals. Using a combination square, mark the outlines of the joists on the ledger, beams, and rim joist.

Nail the joist hangers to the short ledger and rim joist, using a scrap 2 × 8 as a spacer to achieve the correct spread for each hanger.

Cut the joists (G) to length. Insert the joists into the hangers with the crown up, and attach them with joist hanger nails. Align the joists with the marks on the beams and toenail them in place.

INSTALL THE BLOCKING

The ends of the decking boards in the diamond pattern are supported by a row of double blocking at the center of the pattern and a row of single blocking at the edge of the pattern.

To locate the rows of blocking, measure from the inside corner of the house along the long ledger (see Framing Plan, page 260). Drive one screw or nail at 78", and another at 156". Make corresponding marks across from the ledger on the end joist.

Snap chalk lines across the joists, between the ledger and the end joist. The line at 78" is the centerline of the double blocking. The line at 156" is the outer edge of the single blocking. Don't be concerned if the blocking is not directly over the beams.

Cut double blocking pieces from 2 × 8s nailed together with 16d galvanized nails.

Install the blocking by alternating end nailing using galvanized joist hangers.

To achieve the best fit, measure the actual length of the last deck board in each course before cutting.

LAY THE DECKING

Except for the three rows of straight decking at the top of the stairway, the decking is laid in a diamond pattern.

Begin at the center of the diamond pattern, where the double joist and the double blocking intersect. Cut four identical triangles, as large as possible, from 2 × 6" cedar stock.

Drill ⅛" pilot holes in the ends, position the pieces as shown, and attach with 3" deck screws.

To install the remaining courses, measure, cut, drill, and attach the first three boards in each course. Then, measure the actual length of the last board to achieve the best fit. For best results, install the decking course by course. Maintain a ⅛" gap between courses.

Once the diamond decking pattern is complete, cut and install the three remaining deck boards.

BUILD THE STAIRS

For the position of the stairway footings, refer to the Framing Plan on page 260. Locate the footings by extending a 2 × 4 from the deck, perpendicular to the rim joist, dropping a plumb bob, and marking the centerpoints on the ground with stakes.

Dig postholes with a clamshell digger or an auger, and pour footings using the same method as for the deck footings. Insert J-bolts, leaving ¾" to 1" of thread exposed. Allow the concrete to set. Attach metal post anchors.

Cut the stairway posts (K) to length, adding approximately 6" for final trimming. Place the posts in the anchors.

Use a level to ensure that the posts are plumb, and attach the posts to the anchors with 16d galvanized nails.

Cut the stringers (L) to length and use a framing square to mark the rise and run for each step (see Stairway Detail, page 261). Draw the tread outline on each run. Cut the angles at the ends of the stringers with a circular saw. (For a more detailed description of stairway construction, see pages 120 to 137.)

Drill pilot holes and then attach the treads to the stringers, using 1¼" lag screws and angle brackets.

Fasten the stair to the deck with a ratchet wrench, using 4" lag screws.

Position an angle bracket flush with the bottom of each tread outline. Drill ⅛" pilot holes in the stringers, and attach the angle brackets with 1¼" lag screws.

The treads (M) fit between the stringers, and the stringers fit between the stairway posts. Measure and cut the treads (M) to length, 3" shorter than the distance between the stairway posts.

Assemble the stairway upside down on sawhorses. Mark and drill ⅛" pilot holes at the ends of the treads. Position each front tread with its front edge flush to the tread outline, and attach to the angle brackets with ¼ × 1¼" lag screws.

Attach the rear treads in similar fashion, leaving a ⅛" gap between treads.

Position the stairway in place against the edge of the deck, making sure the top of the stringer is flush with the surface of the deck. From underneath the deck, drill ¼" pilot holes through the rim joist into the stringers. Attach the stringers to the rim joist with 4" lag screws, using a ratchet wrench.

To fasten the stairway to the stair posts, drill two ¼" pilot holes through each stringer into a post. Counterbore the pilot holes ½" deep with a 1" spade bit, and use a ratchet wrench to drive 4" lag screws with washers. Seal the screw heads with silicone caulk.

INSTALL THE DECK RAILING

Cut the railing posts (N) and balusters (O) to length (see Railing Detail, page 261) with a power miter saw or circular saw. Cut the tops square and the bottoms at 45° angles.

Drill two ¼" pilot holes at the bottom end of each railing post, positioned so the lag screws will attach to the rim joist. Counterbore the holes ½" deep with a 1" spade bit.

Drill two ⅛" pilot holes near the bottom of each baluster, spaced 4" apart. At the top of each baluster, drill a pair of ⅛" pilot holes spaced 1½" apart.

With the help of a combination square, draw the outlines of the railing posts around the perimeter of the deck. The posts at the corner must be spaced so there is less than 4" between them.

Hold each railing post in its position, with the end 1½" above the bottom edge of the deck platform (see Railing Detail, page 261). Make sure the post is plumb, and insert an awl through the counterbored holes to mark pilot hole locations on the deck.

Set the post aside and drill ¼" pilot holes at the marks. Attach the railing posts to the deck with ⅜ × 4" lag screws and washers. Seal the screw heads with silicone caulk.

Cut the top rails (P) to length with the ends mitered at 45° where they meet in the corner. Attach them to the railing posts with 3" deck screws, keeping the edges of the rails flush with the tops of the posts.

To position the balusters, measure the total distance between two railing posts, and mark the centerpoint on the top rail. The two railing sections on the long side of this deck will have a baluster at the centerpoint; the two railing sections on the stairway side will have a space at the centerpoint. *Note: If the dimensions of your deck vary from the plan, calculate whether you will have a baluster or a space at the center of each section.*

Cut a spacer slightly less than 4" wide. Start at the center of each railing section, and position either a baluster or a space over the line. Measure out from the center both ways, marking the outlines of the balusters on the top rail. The end spaces may be narrow, but they will be symmetrical.

With the stairway top rail cut to size and installed, attach the railing cap with deck screws.

To install the balusters, begin next to a railing post and make sure the first baluster is plumb. Install the remaining balusters, holding each one tight against the spacer and flush with the top rail. Attach the balusters with 2½" deck screws.

Cut the deck railing cap (Q) to length, with the ends mitered at 45° where they meet in the corner. Position the railing cap sections so the inside edge overhangs the inside edge of the top rail by ¼". Attach the cap with 3" deck screws.

INSTALL THE STAIRWAY RAILING

Determine the exact size and shape of the stairway top rail. Tack a cedar 2 × 4 across the faces of the stairway post and deck post with 10d galvanized nails. Make sure the angle of the 2 × 4 is parallel with the angle of the stringer below.

On the back side of the 2 × 4, mark the outline of the deck railing post and the end of the deck top rail. On the stairway post, mark a diagonal cutoff line at the top edge of the 2 × 4. At the lower end of the 2 × 4, use a level to mark a plumb cutoff line directly above the end of the stringer.

Remove the 2 × 4 and make the cuts.

Drill ⅛" pilot holes through the stairway top rail. Place in position and attach with 2½" deck screws.

To trim the top ends of the stairway balusters, hold a baluster against the stairway post and draw a diagonal cut line along the top edge of the rail. Trim the baluster. Using this baluster as a template, mark and cut the remaining stairway balusters.

Install the stairway balusters with 2½" deck screws, using the same procedure as for the deck balusters.

Measure the railing caps for the stairway. Cut the caps to size, with the upper ends beveled to fit against the deck posts, and the lower ends beveled to align with the end of the top rail. Install the caps by drilling ⅛" pilot holes and attaching them with 2½" deck screws.

After the top rail and balusters have been installed, install the railing cap with its inside edge overhanging the inside face of the top rail by ¼".

Island Deck

An island deck can transform any area of your yard into a virtual oasis. Since it's not attached to your house, you can position your island deck wherever you like—to capitalize on a spectacular view or to catch the cool afternoon breeze in a shady glen.

Accessible and inviting with its three-sided landing, this deck welcomes visitors of all ages. And it can readily serve as a cornerstone for a total landscaping plan; one that will make your entire yard a more comfortable and attractive space for enjoying the great outdoors.

The perfect place to visit when you need to relax.

Cutaway View

Note: Sandwiched post/beam connections are no longer allowed in some regions. Check with your local building department.

Overall size:
14'-1½" Long
14'-1½" Wide
2'-4" High

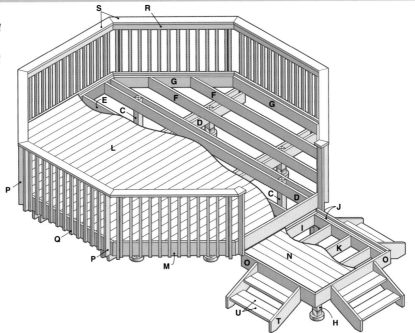

Supplies

10"-diameter footing forms (8)
8"-diameter footing forms (4)
J-bolts (12)
6 × 6" metal post anchors (8)
4 × 4" metal post anchors (4)
90° 2 × 8" joist hangers (10)
45° 2 × 8" joist hangers (8)
Joist ties (16)
Post-beam caps (4)

Joist hanger nails
1½ × 10" angle brackets (12)
3" galvanized deck screws
¼ × 1¼" galvanized lag screws and washers (96)
16d galvanized box nails
½ × 7" carriage bolts, washers, and nuts (16)
⅜ × 5" lag screws and washers (32)
Concrete as required

Lumber List

Qty.	Size	Material	Part
4	2 × 4" × 16'	Pine	Site chooser sides (A)
2	2 × 4" × 12'	Pine	Site chooser diagonals (B)
3	6 × 6 × 8'	Trtd. lumber	Deck posts (C)
1	4 × 4" × 8'	Trtd. lumber	Landing posts (H)
10	2 × 8" × 14'	Trtd. lumber	Beam boards (D), Long joists (E)
2	2 × 8" × 12'	Trtd. lumber	Mitered joists (F)
6	2 × 8" × 10'	Trtd. lumber	Mitered joists (F), Inner rim joists (I), Outer rim joists (J), Landing joists (K)
9	2 × 8" × 6'	Trtd. lumber	Deck rim joists (G), Landing joists (K)
25	2 × 6" × 14'	Cedar	Deck decking (L), Railing cap (S)
23	2 × 6" × 14'	Cedar	Deck decking (L), Railing cap (S)

Qty.	Size	Material	Part
7	2 × 6" × 12'	Cedar	Deck decking (L)
13	2 × 6" × 10'	Cedar	Deck decking (L), Landing decking (N), Treads (U)
4	2 × 6" × 8'	Cedar	Deck decking (L)
11	2 × 10" × 6'	Cedar	Deck face boards (M), Landing face boards (O)
8	2 × 4" × 8'	Cedar	Railing posts (P)
42	2 × 2" × 8'	Cedar	Balusters (Q)
7	2 × 4" × 6'	Cedar	Top rail (R)
3	2 × 10" × 6'	Cedar	Stringers (T)

Framing Plan

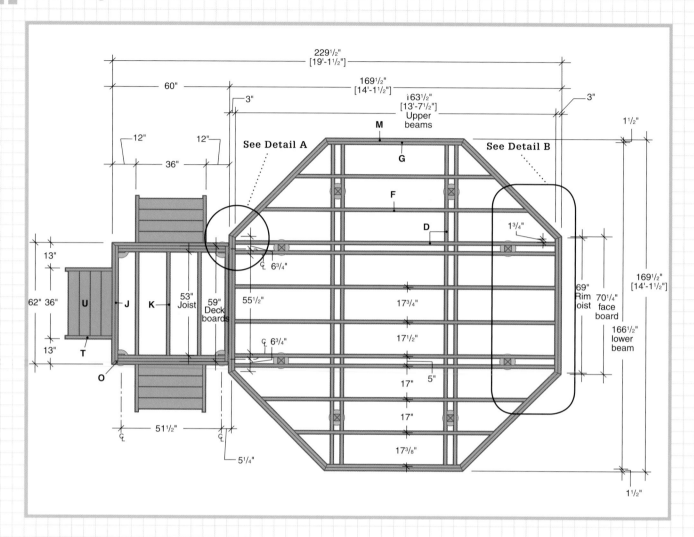

229½"
[19'-1½"]

169½"
[14'-1½"]

i63½"
[13'-7½"]
Upper beams

60"

3"

3"

1½"

12"

12"

M

36"

See Detail A

G

See Detail B

F

13"

D

1¾"

169½"
[14'-1½"]

62" 36" U J K 53" 59" 55½" 6¾" 17¾" 69" 70¼" 166½"
Joist Deck Rim face lower
boards 6¾" 17½" oist board beam

13"

T

5"

17"

O

5"

17"

51½"

17"

5¼"

17⅜"

1½"

Elevation

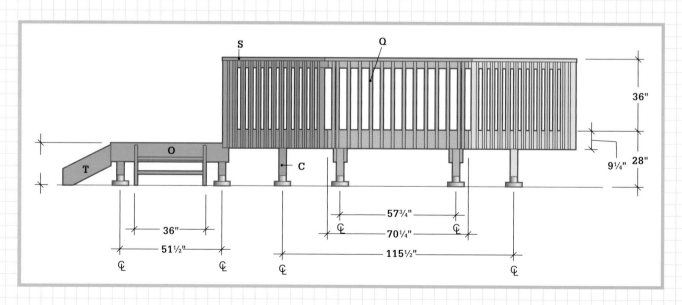

S

Q

36"

O

C

9¼" 28"

T

36"

57¾"

51½"

70¼"

115½"

Detail A

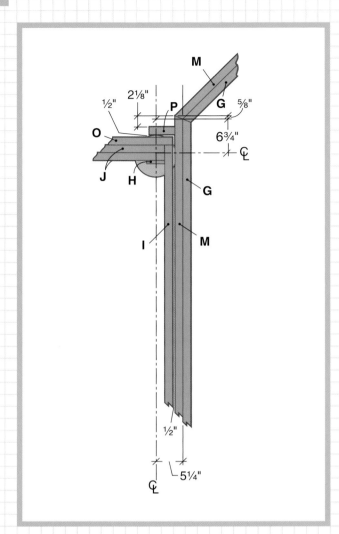

Detail B

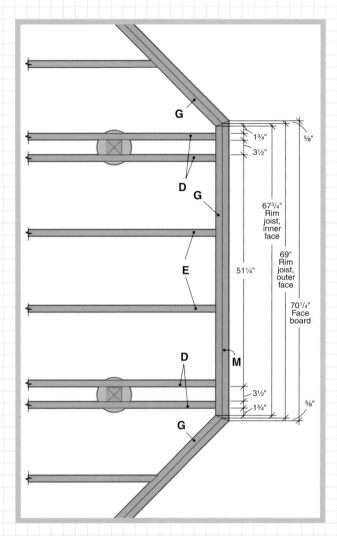

Landing & Stairway Detail

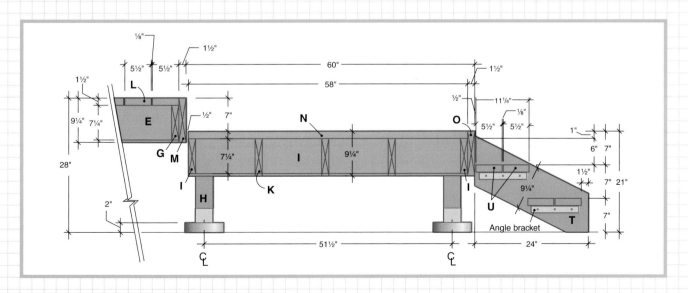

Site Chooser Detail

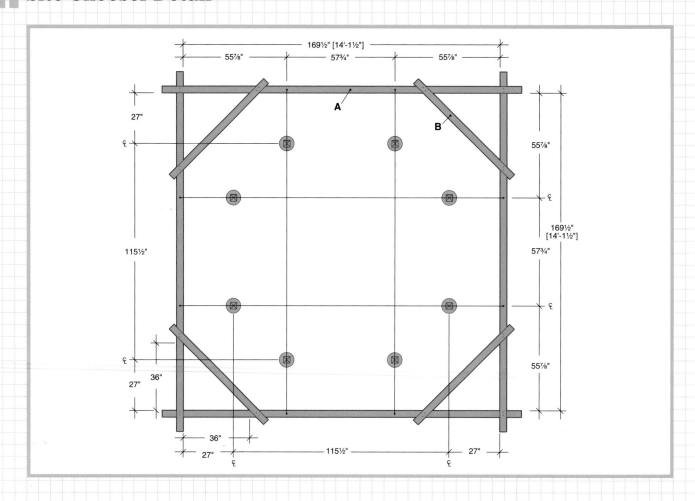

Railing Detail

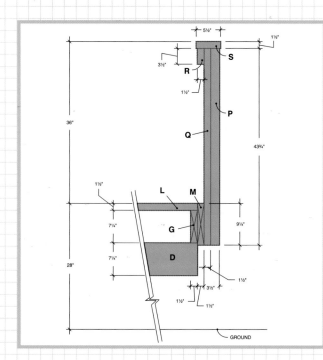

Face Board Detail

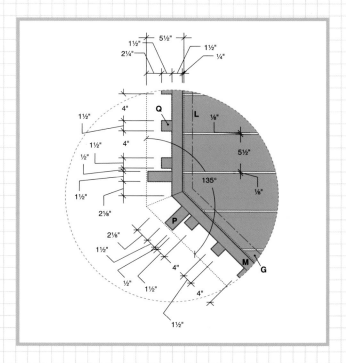

How to Build an Island Deck

POSITION THE DECK

Measure, mark, and cut to length the site chooser frame (A) and diagonal braces (B), (see Site Chooser Detail, page 270).

Fasten the frame together with 3" deck screws, and check for squareness by measuring corner to corner. Adjust the frame so measurements are identical, and attach the diagonal braces with deck screws.

With a helper, move the site chooser to select the exact deck location. When you've established the deck position, set the site chooser on sawhorses and tack or clamp in place to conveniently find the footing locations.

LOCATE THE FOOTINGS

Mark the footing centerlines on the frame and stretch mason's string across the site from mark to mark. Measure along the strings, marking the footing locations with tape.

Drop a plumb bob from each marked location, and drive stakes into the ground to mark the centers of the deck footings.

POUR THE FOOTINGS

Remove the mason's strings and dig the footing holes, using a clamshell digger or power auger. Pour 2" to 3" of loose gravel into each hole for drainage. Make sure hole dimensions comply with your local building code, which may require flaring the base to 12".

Cut concrete tube forms to length, using a reciprocating saw or handsaw. Insert tubes into holes, leaving 2" of tube above ground level. Pack soil around tubes and fill tubes with concrete. Tamp with a long stick or rod to eliminate air gaps.

Screed the concrete flush, using a straight 2 × 4, and insert a J-bolt into each footing, leaving ¾" to 1" of the thread exposed. Retie the mason's strings and position the J-bolt at the center of the footing, using a plumb bob as a guide. Clean bolt threads before concrete sets.

SET THE DECK POSTS

Lay a straight 2 × 4 flat across each pair of footings, with one edge tight against the J-bolts. Draw a line across the top of each footing to help orient the post anchors.

Place a metal post anchor on each footing, centering it over the J-bolt and squaring it with the reference line. Thread a nut over each J-bolt and tighten the post anchors in place.

Cut the deck posts (C), several inches long to allow

for final trimming. Set the posts in the anchors, brace the taller posts plumb, and nail the posts in place.

Establish the height of the taller posts by measuring up 26½" from ground level and marking one post. Using a mason's string and a line level, transfer this mark to the remaining tall posts. To establish the height of the lower beam posts, measure down 7¼" from the first line and transfer a level mark to the four lower posts.

INSTALL THE DECK BEAMS

This deck uses two sets of beams. The lower beams are three inches longer than the upper beams, because the rim joists rest on them. The lower beams support the upper beams and the deck platform.

Measure, mark, and cut the four lower beam

Use the site chooser to experiment with possible deck locations and to find the site you like best.

Locate the deck footings by stretching mason's strings across the site chooser, marking footing locations with tape, and dropping a plumb bob from each mark.

(continued)

boards (D) to length. Mark the post locations on the tops and sides of the lower beams, using a combination square as a guide.

Position the lower beams crown-side-up on their posts. Make sure they are level, and fasten them with deck screws. Trim the tops of the posts flush with a reciprocating saw or a handsaw.

Drill two ½" holes through the beams at each post. Securely attach the lower beams with joist ties, carriage bolts, and washers, using a ratchet wrench.

Measure, mark, and cut the upper beams (D) to length. Mark post locations and attach, following the same steps as for the lower beams.

INSTALL THE RIM JOISTS

Cut four of the eight rim joists (G) to length (see Detail B, page 269), using a circular saw. Make 22½° miter cuts on the ends.

Attach one rim joist to each end of the upper beams (see Detail B, page 269) by nailing through the rim joist into the beams with box nails. Toenail the remaining two rim joists to the tops of the lower beams.

Verify the measurements of the remaining rim joists, cut to length, miter the ends at 22½°, and install. At the corners, drill pairs of ⅛" pilot holes, and fasten the adjacent rim joists to each other with deck screws.

POUR LANDING FOOTINGS & INSTALL POSTS

Locate the landing footings by stretching a mason's string out from the rim joist to a batterboard, according to the measurements on the Framing Plan, page 268, and Detail A, page 269. Make sure the strings are perpendicular to the rim joist and are parallel with each other.

Mark the footing locations with tape. Use a plumb bob and stakes to transfer the locations to the ground. Remove the mason's strings and dig holes for the footings. Pour 2" to 3" of loose gravel into each hole for drainage.

Insert tubes into holes. Leave 2" of tube above ground level, pack soil around tubes, and fill tubes with concrete. Tamp the concrete to eliminate air gaps. Screed the tops flush and insert a J-bolt into each footing, leaving ¾" to 1" of the thread exposed. Retie the mason's strings and position the J-bolt at the centerpoint of the footing, using a plumb bob. Clean bolt threads before concrete sets.

Install post anchors, cut the landing posts to length (see Detail, page 269), and attach the posts to the post anchors.

INSTALL LANDING BEAMS & RIM JOISTS

Attach post-beam caps to the tops of the landing posts. Verify size, mark, and cut the beam boards (J) and rim joists (I) to length. Hold one pair of beam boards together, then measure and mark the post-beam cap locations on the tops and sides of the boards, using a combination square. Repeat for the second pair of boards.

Place beams, crown side up, into the post-beam caps and align. Drill pilot holes and fasten the caps to the beams with deck screws.

Position the rim joists flush with the side and top of the beams (see Detail A, page 269), drill ⅛" pilot holes through the rim joists, and fasten with deck screws.

INSTALL DECK & LANDING JOISTS

For the deck, the inner joists are installed with joist hangers and toenailed to the tops of the lower beams. This deck uses 90° joist hangers for the landing and for the two deck joists between the upper beams. For the angled deck joists, we used 45° joist hangers.

Using the plan, measure along the deck rim joists and lower beams, marking where joists attach. Draw the outline of each joist on the beams, using a combination square as a guide.

Measure, mark, and cut lumber for long joists (E) and mitered joists (F), using a circular saw. Mark the ends of the mitered joists with a 22½° angle, using a speed square, and cut the ends.

Place joists in hangers with crown side up, and attach with nails. Align joists with the outlines on the top edges of the lower beams and toenail in place.

Measure and mark locations of landing joists (K) on landing beams. Position joist hangers and attach with nails. Install landing joists and nail in place.

LAY THE DECK DECKING

Measure, cut, and position the first row of decking (L) next to the landing, and attach by driving a pair of deck screws into each joist. Position the remaining decking boards so ends overhang the rim joists, leaving a ⅛" gap between the boards to provide for drainage. Attach boards to each joist with a pair of deck screws.

Snap a chalk line on the decking to mark a line flush with the outside edge of the deck, and trim the deck boards with a circular saw.

INSTALL THE FACE BOARDS

Measure, mark, and cut deck face boards (M). Miter-cut the ends at 22½°. Position face boards flush with decking and attach to rim joists, using deck screws.

Verify the measurements, mark, and cut the landing face boards (O) to length. Position top edges flush with decking, and attach to landing beams and front rim joist, using deck screws.

BUILD THE RAILING

Measure, mark, and cut the railing posts (P) to length (see Railing Detail, page 269). At the bottom of each post, counterbore two holes ½" deep, using a spade bit slightly larger than the diameter of the washers. Position posts (see Face Board Detail, above), mark and drill pilot holes in deck, and attach to the face board and rim joist, using lag screws.

Cut each top rail section (R) the same length as the face board below it. Miter the ends of each section at 22½°. Fasten the top rails to the posts with screws.

Measure, mark, and cut railing balusters (Q) to length. Drill ⅛" pilot holes in the balusters, and attach them to the face boards and the top rails with screws.

Cut the railing cap sections (S), to length with 22½° miters where the ends meet. Attach to the posts and top rail with deck screws.

BUILD THE STAIRWAYS

Measure, mark, and cut the stringers (T) to size. Using a framing square, lay out the top step with a 6" rise and 12" run. Extend the rise line to both edges of the stringer, and cut along this line.

Lay out the bottom step with a 7" rise and a 12¾" run. At the end of the run, draw a perpendicular line 7" long and make a mark. Draw another perpendicular line to the bottom edge of the stringer and cut to size.

Position the angle brackets in place and attach to the stringers, using 1¼" lag screws.

Measure, mark, and cut the treads (U) to length, and attach to the stringers with lag screws through the angle brackets, leaving a ⅛" gap between treads.

Install the stairways by propping them in position against the landing, and drilling ¼" pilot holes through the rim joists and face boards into the top end of the stringers. Attach with a pair of lag screws at each stringer.

After installing the stairways, cut the landing decking (N) to length and attach with deck screws.

Locate the landing footings with mason's string and a plumb bob.

Drill ⅛" pilot holes, then screw the top rail sections together where they meet at the corners.

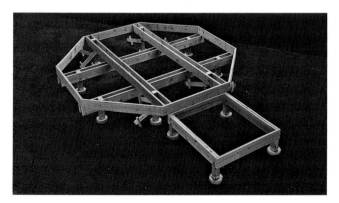

Measure, mark, and cut the landing beams. Attach them to the landing posts, using post-beam caps.

After attaching angle brackets, turn stringers upside down and install treads, using 1¼" lag screws.

Wraparound Deck

By wrapping around an outside corner of your house, this versatile deck increases your living space and lets you take advantage of views in several directions. The plan also creates two symmetrical areas for sitting or relaxing, providing space for two distinct activities. Our plan also calls for a front stairway for easy access to your yard or garden. The horizontal rails and notched posts provide striking visual elements that enhance the deck's overall design and add to its intimate nature.

Combine multiple seating possibilities with an expansive view.

Cutaway View

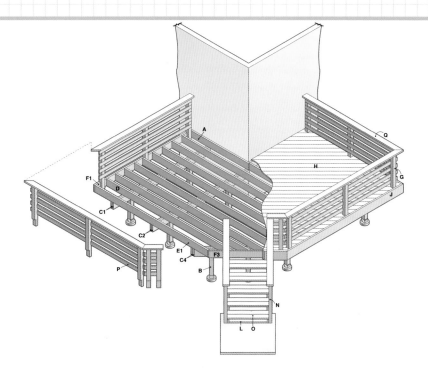

Overall size:
16'-0" Long
16'-0" Wide
3'-6" High

Supplies

10"-diameter footing forms (8)
J-bolts (8)
6 × 6" metal post anchors (8)
Post-beam caps (8)
90° 2 × 8" joist hangers (26)
45° 2 × 8" joist hangers (3)
1½ × 1½" galvanized metal angle brackets
    (26)
Joist hanger nails
⅜ × 4" lag screws and washers (20)
⅜ × 3" lag screws and washers (32)
6 × 30" mending plate (1)
Silicone caulk (3 tubes)
3" masonry screws
3" galvanized deck screws
1½" galvanized deck screws
⅝" galvanized screws
Concrete as required

Lumber List

Qty.	Size	Material	Part
9	2 × 8" × 16'	Trtd. Lumber	Joists (D)
6	2 × 8" × 12'	Trtd. Lumber	Ledgers (A), Beam boards (C), End joist (E), Rim joist (F)
13	2 × 8" × 10'	Trtd. Lumber	Beam boards (C), Joists (D), End joist (E), Rim joists (F), Lower gusset (L)
1	2 × 6" × 4'	Trtd. Lumber	Stairway nailer (I)
1	2 × 4" × 4'	Trtd. Lumber	Upper gusset (L)
3	6 × 6" × 8'	Trtd. Lumber	Deck posts (B)
9	4 × 4" × 8'	Cedar	Deck railing posts (G), Stairway railing posts (N)
28	5/4 × 6" × 16'	Cedar	Decking (H)
2	2 × 10" × 12'	Cedar	Face boards (J)
2	2 × 10" × 10'	Cedar	Face boards (J)
1	2 × 10" × 6'	Cedar	Face boards (J)
1	2 × 12" × 12'	Cedar	Stringers (K)
5	2 × 6" × 12'	Cedar	Railing cap (Q)
5	2 × 6" × 8'	Cedar	Treads (O)
10	1 × 4" × 12'	Cedar	Rails (P)
11	1 × 4" × 10'	Cedar	Rails (P)
8	1 × 4" × 6'	Cedar	Rails (P)

How to Build a Wraparound Deck

ATTACH THE LEDGERS

Draw a level outline on the siding to show where the ledgers and the adjacent end joist and rim joist will fit against the house.

Position the top edge of the ledgers so that the surface of the decking boards will be 1" below the indoor floor level. This height difference prevents rainwater or melted snow from seeping into the house. Draw the outline long enough to accommodate the thickness of rim joist F-1 and end joist E-2.

Cut out the siding along the outline with a circular saw. To keep the blade from cutting the sheathing underneath the siding, set the blade depth to the same thickness as the siding. Finish the corners of the cutout with a chisel, holding the beveled side in to ensure a straight cut. Cut galvanized flashing to the length of the cutout, using metal snips, and slide the flashing up under the siding.

Measure and cut the ledgers (A) to length from pressure-treated lumber, using a circular saw. Remember, the ledger boards should be shorter than the overall length of the cutouts. Position the ledgers in the cutout, underneath the flashing, and brace them in place. Fasten them temporarily with deck screws.

Drill pairs of ¼" pilot holes through the ledger and sheathing and into the house header joist at 2' intervals. Counterbore each pilot hole ½" deep, using a 1" spade bit. Attach the ledgers to the wall with ⅜ × 4" lag screws and washers, using a ratchet wrench.

Apply a thick bead of silicone caulk between the siding and the flashing. Also seal the lag screw heads and any gaps between the wall and the ledger.

POUR THE FOOTINGS

Referring to the Footing Location Diagram (page 277), stretch mason's strings across the site, using 2 × 4 batterboards. Check the mason's strings for square, using the 3-4-5 triangle method. From the point where each string meets the ledger, measure 3' along the ledger and make a mark. Next, measure 4' out along the mason's string and mark with tape. The distance between the points on the ledger and the string should be 5'. If not, adjust the mason's strings accordingly. Measure along the strings to locate the centerpoints of the footings. Mark the locations with tape.

Drop a plumb bob at the tape locations, and drive stakes into the ground to mark the centerpoints of the footings. Remove the mason's strings and dig holes

Use a speed square to mark a 22½° miter cut where the ends of beams C-3 and C-4 fit together.

for the footings, using a clamshell digger or power auger. Pour 2" to 3" of loose gravel into each hole for drainage. Make certain the hole dimensions comply with your local building code, which may require flaring the footings at the base. Cut the footing forms to length, using a reciprocating saw or handsaw. Insert the forms into the holes, leaving 2" of each form above grade. Pack soil around the forms.

Fill the forms with concrete and tamp the concrete with a long stick to eliminate any air pockets. Screed the tops flush with a flat 2 × 4. Insert a J-bolt into each footing, leaving ¾" to 1" of thread exposed.

Retie the mason's strings and drop a plumb bob to position each J-bolt at the exact center of the footing. Clean the bolt threads before the concrete sets.

SET THE DECK POSTS

Start by laying a long, straight 2 × 4 flat across each pair of footings. With one edge tight against the J-bolts, draw a reference line across each footing.

Place a metal post anchor on each footing, center it over the J-bolt, and square it with the reference line. Thread a nut over each J-bolt and tighten each of the post anchors in place.

Cut the posts (C) to their approximate length, adding several inches for final trimming. Place the posts in the anchors and tack them into place with one nail each.

With a level as a guide, use braces and stakes to plumb the posts. Once the posts are plumb, finish nailing them to the anchors. To determine the height of the posts, make a mark on the house, 7¼" down from the bottom edge of the ledger. Use a straight 2 × 4 and a level to extend this line across a post. Transfer this line to the remaining posts. Cut the posts off with a reciprocating saw or a handsaw and attach post-beam caps to the tops, using 8d nails.

INSTALL THE BEAMS

Cut the beams from 2 × 10" lumber, adding several inches to each beam for final trimming. Position the beam boards (C) so the crowns face the same direction, and fasten them together with 10d galvanized nails spaced every 16".

Position beams C-1 and C-2 in their post-beam caps and attach them with nails. Mark and cut the angled end of beam C-3 by mitering it at 22½°. Position the beam in the post caps.

Make a 22½° miter cut at one end of beam C-4 to form a 45° corner with beam C-3. Leave the other end long for final trimming. Place beam C-4 in the post-beam caps. Fit the beams tightly together, fasten them with 3" deck screws, and attach them to the post caps with 8d nails.

INSTALL THE JOISTS

Referring to the Framing Plan on page 276, cut rim joist F-1 to final length, and cut end joist E-1 generously long, to allow for final trimming.

Fasten one end of rim joist F-1 to the ledger with 16d galvanized nails. Rest end joist E-1 in place on beams C-1 and C-2. Fasten F-1 and E-1 together with deck screws. Use a framing square to finalize the location of E-1 on the beams. Mark the beams and trim them to length. Toenail E-1 in place on the beams.

Cut end joist E-2 to length. Install it by nailing it to the end of the ledger, checking for square, and toenailing

Mark the three remaining inside joists for cutting by snapping a chalk line. Brace and miter-cut the three inside joists.

it to the top of beam C-3. Trim the beam to length. Mark the outlines of the inner joists (D) on the ledger, beams and rim joist F-1 (see Framing Plan, page 276), using a tape measure and a combination square.

Attach joist hangers to the ledger and rim joist F-1 with 1¼" joist hanger nails, using a scrap 2 × 8 as a spacer to achieve the correct spread for each hanger. *Note: Spacing between the joists is irregular to accommodate the installation of railing posts.*

Place the inside joists in the hangers on the ledger and on rim joist F-1, crown up, and attach them with 1¼" joist hanger nails. Be sure to use all the nail holes in the hangers. Toenail the joists to the beams and leave the joists long for final trimming.

Mark the final length of the inside joists by making a line across the tops of the joists from the end of end joist E-2. Check for square. Brace the inside joists by tacking a board across their edges for stability. Cut them to length with a circular saw.

Cut rim joist F-2 long to allow for final trimming, and nail into position with 16d galvanized nails.

To mark the remaining joists for trimming at a 45° angle, make a mark 139" from the 90° corner on end joist E-1. Make a second mark 139" from the other 90° corner along rim joist F-2. The distance between these two points should be at least 70". If necessary, move the line back until it measures 70". Regardless of the overall dimensions of your deck, this length will ensure adequate space for mounting the railing posts at the top of the stairway.

Mark the last three joists for cutting by snapping a chalk line between the marked points on end joist E-1 and rim joist F-2. Transfer the cut marks to the faces of the joists with a combination square, and cut the miters with a circular saw.

Measure, cut, and attach rim joist F-3 across the angle with deck screws.

Fit beam C-4 tightly against beam C-3 and attach the two beams to each other with deck screws.

(continued)

Drill pilot holes through the posts and into the rim joists, and attach the posts with lag screws. Note the unnotched stairway post.

INSTALL THE RAILING POSTS

Cut the railing posts (G) to size and notch the lower ends to fit around the rim joists (see Railing Detail, page 277).

Clamp all but two of the posts together to lay out and cut ¾" × 3½" notches, or dadoes, for the horizontal rails. *Note: The posts at the stairway are not notched for rails.*

Cut the dadoes by making a series of parallel ¾"-deep cuts within each 3½" space, about ¼" apart, with a circular saw. Knock out the waste wood between the cuts, using a hammer. Then, chisel smooth the bottom of each dado.

To locate the railing posts on the diagonal corner, find the centerline of rim joist F-3 and measure 18" in both directions. These points are the inner faces of the railing posts and the outer faces of the stringers. Drill ¼" pilot holes through the railing posts into the rim joist, and secure the posts with lag screws.

To position the corner railing posts, measure 3" both ways from the outside corners of rim joist F-3. Predrill the posts, and use a ratchet wrench to attach them to the rim joists with lag screws.

Use the Framing Plan, page 276, and the Corner Post Detail, page 277, to locate the remaining railing posts.

INSTALL THE DECKING

If possible, buy decking boards that are long enough to span the deck.

Measure, mark, and cut the decking (H) to size, making notches to fit around the railing posts. Position the first board above the stairway, and attach it by driving a pair of deck screws into each joist.

Position the remaining decking boards so that the ends overhang the deck, leaving a ⅛" gap between the boards to allow for drainage.

Where more than one board is required to span the deck, cut the ends at 45° angles and make the joint at the center of a joist.

Snap a chalk line flush with the edge of the deck, and cut off the overhanging ends of the deck boards with a circular saw set for a 1½"-deep cut.

INSTALL THE NAILER & FACE BOARDS

Measure, mark, and cut the stairway nailer (I) to size and attach it to the rim joist with a mending plate and deck screws (see Stairway Detail, page 277).

Measure, mark, and cut the face boards (J) to length, making 45° miter cuts at the right angle corners and 22½° miter cuts at the stairway corners. Attach the face boards to the rim and end joists with pairs of deck screws at 2' intervals.

BUILD THE STAIRWAY

Lay out and cut the stringers (K) to size, according to the Stairway Detail, page 277. The center stringer is notched at the top and bottom to fit around the gussets. Mark the rises and runs with a framing square. Cut the notches with a circular saw, using a reciprocating saw or handsaw to finish the corners.

Measure, mark, and cut the gussets (L) to length. Assemble the stairway framework by nailing the gussets in place between the outer stringers with 16d nails. Turn the framework upside down and attach the center stringer by nailing through the gussets.

Position the framework against the deck, and attach with deck screws driven through the upper gusset into the face board and nailer. Drill pilot holes

Cut the notches for the first decking board and position it above the stairway.

Drill ⅛" pilot holes through the treads to prevent splitting. Then, attach the treads to the stringers with deck screws, using a power driver.

Clamp the long rails, mark the ends, and transfer the lines across the face of the board with a combination square to ensure a tight-fitting 22½° miter with the short rail.

through the lower gusset into the concrete pad; attach with masonry screws.

Cut the stairway railing posts (N) to length. To install the railing posts, clamp them in place against the stringers, drill pilot holes through the stringers into the posts, and attach the posts with ⅜ × 4" lag screws.

Measure, mark and cut the treads (O) to length. For the bottom treads, use a piece of railing post scrap to trace a line for the notch. Then, cut the notch with a circular saw. Attach the treads to the stringers with deck screws.

BUILD THE RAILING

Measure and cut to length the 10' rails, each with one end mitered at 45°. Install the rails, using 1½" deck screws. Miter one end of the long rails at 45°. Leave the other end long for final trimming. Clamp each long rail in place and use a straightedge to mark cut lines at the angled corner). Transfer this line to the face of each rail, using a combination square. Remove the rails and miter-cut the ends for the angled corners at 22½°. Reposition the rails and attach them to the railing posts with 1½" deck screws. Measure, mark, and cut the short rails to length with one end mitered at 22½° and the other end cut square.

Fasten the ends of the short rails to the railing posts above the stairway with angle brackets. Use ⅝" galvanized screws to attach the brackets to the rails and 1½" deck screws to attach them to the posts. Attach them to the notched post as well, using 1½" deck screws.

Measure, mark, and cut the deck railing cap (Q), and install it with 3" deck screws.

Use angle brackets to attach the stairway railing pieces and angled rails. To attach the brackets to the rails, use ⅝" galvanized screws.

BUILD THE STAIRWAY RAILING

Mark and cut the stairway posts to length. Measure, mark, and cut the stairway railing caps (see Stairway Detail, page 277). Place a cedar 2 × 6 on top of the stairway posts, mark the angles for the ends, and cut to length, allowing for a 1" overhang at the end of the stairway.

Install the stairway railing caps with 3" deck screws. To cut the stairway rails, hold each one tight against the bottom of the cap and mark the ends.

Cut the rails to length so that they fit tight between the posts. To install the rails, mark the positions of the rails on the posts and attach them with angle brackets, using ⅝" screws and 1½" deck screws.

Angled Deck

Expand your living space with style. This attractive deck makes creative use of simple geometry to achieve both practicality and pizzazz.

The railing adds interest with its combination of vertical balusters, horizontal rails, and shaped railing posts. And the straight staircase—anchored to a concrete pad for stability—provides direct, convenient access.

Though designed for construction at medium height on level ground, this deck uses heavy-duty posts, beams, joists, and footings. By simply lengthening posts and modifying the stairway, it's readily adaptable for installation at a higher level or on a sloped site.

Give yourself a commanding view from this unique angled deck.